NEW DIRECTIONS FOR MENTAL HEALTH SERVICES

H. Richard Lamb, *University of Southern California*
EDITOR-IN-CHIEF

Clinical Studies in Case Management

Joel Kanter
Mount Vernon Center
for Community Mental Health

EDITOR

Number 65, Spring 1995

JOSSEY-BASS PUBLISHERS
San Francisco

CLINICAL STUDIES IN CASE MANAGEMENT
Joel Kanter (ed.)
New Directions for Mental Health Services, no. 65
H. *Richard Lamb*, Editor-in-Chief

Microfilm copies of issues and articles are available in 16mm and 35mm, as well as microfiche in 105mm, through University Microfilms Inc., 300 North Zeeb Road, Ann Arbor, Michigan 48106-1346.

LC 87-646993   ISSN 0193-9416   ISBN 0-7879-9921-0

NEW DIRECTIONS FOR MENTAL HEALTH SERVICES is part of The Jossey-Bass Social and Behavioral Science Series and is published quarterly by Jossey-Bass Inc., Publishers, 350 Sansome Street, San Francisco, California 94104-1342.

EDITORIAL CORRESPONDENCE should be sent to the Editor-in-Chief, H. Richard Lamb, Department of Psychiatry and the Behavioral Sciences, U.S.C. School of Medicine, 1934 Hospital Place, Los Angeles, California 90033-1071.

Cover photograph by Wernher Krutein/PHOTOVAULT © 1990.

Manufactured in the United States of America. Nearly all Jossey-Bass books, jackets, and periodicals are printed on recycled paper that contains at least 50 percent recycled waste, including 10 percent postconsumer waste. Many of our materials are also printed with vegetable-based inks; during the printing process, these inks emit fewer volatile organic compounds (VOCs) than petroleum-based inks. VOCs contribute to the formation of smog.

Contents

Editor's Notes

In contrast with other areas of mental health practice, case management policy has developed before case management practice. Without the benefit of experience as case managers, policy makers are mandating practice methods, caseload sizes, and staffing patterns. Similarly, models of case management practice have been rushed into print before being adequately tested, either clinically or empirically (Harris and Bergman, 1993). Often filled with the buzzwords of the moment, the case management literature often fails to convey the day-to-day efforts of case managers and other mental health professionals to help persons with severe mental illnesses survive, and even thrive, in their communities.

This volume, a collection of six extended case reports, is an attempt to describe the "marathon" of the case management process as it unfolds over many years. Although we are all aware that many clients struggle with their illnesses for decades, case management is often viewed as a predictable, gradual, and linear process (Kanter, 1985). The ubiquitous problem-focused treatment planning process implies that applying Intervention A to Client B for ninety days will magically alleviate years of suffering. The work of John Strauss, Courtney Harding, and their associates (Strauss, Hafez, Lieberman, and Harding, 1985; Harding and Strauss, 1985; Harding and others, 1987) has empirically challenged these assumptions, providing us with conceptual tools for understanding the often surprising ways that our clients recover from their illnesses and adapt to life in the community. Reminiscent of Schulz and Kilgalen's work from an earlier era (1969), the in-depth case reports in this volume, with the clients' identities concealed with pseudonyms and altered biographical details, illustrate these processes in a more personal way.

In selecting the case reports and contributors in this volume, I sought case reports of interventions that lasted at least three years and that resulted in a demonstrably positive outcome. The authors of these reports have worked with the clients they present between three and a half and twelve years, and often have considerable information about prior interventions. All report clearly positive outcomes except David Mays, who poignantly presents ten years of assertive interventions with a dually diagnosed client.

To provide a historical and cultural perspective, I obtained permission to republish an unusual case report by Marjorie Sheppard. First published in a British social work journal in 1964, Sheppard's case study describes ten years of involvement with an older, paranoid woman who was reluctant to become a client or patient. Straightforwardly raising the question of whether "casework" or case management is merely a form of friendship, Sheppard's presentation reminds us that what we now call "case management" was not invented fifteen years ago by the National Institute of Mental Health's Community Support

Program, but has been practiced by social workers for many years on both sides of the Atlantic (Knee, 1955). Sheppard's case study appears as Chapter One.

I also sought to present a variety of clinical problems. David Mays (Chapter Three) and John Dende and John Kline (Chapter Four) present reports of homeless, dually diagnosed clients in urban settings, though with very different treatment approaches. In contrast, I (Chapter Two) present the story of a treatment-resistant young woman with schizophrenia who benefited from the care and support of a loving family.

Joseph Walsh (Chapter Five) and Barbara Zimmann Caceres, Jack Barber, Carolyn Maurer, and I (Chapter Six) both present reports of women with histories of childhood sexual abuse and diagnoses of borderline personality disorder. Although many discussions of case management focus on clients who are homeless, dually diagnosed, or carry a diagnosis of schizophrenia, these clients are examples of the often nonpsychotic persons who seem to require the most attention from our community support systems and are often the most frequent recidivists; by the age of twenty-five, each of these clients had been hospitalized over twenty times. With considerable personal resources—both have been employed for most of their lives—these clients required a genuine integration of psychological and environmental interventions, as neither conventional psychotherapy nor case management support would have sufficed. In the report presented by Caceres and her colleagues, successful intervention required an extended stay in a public psychiatric hospital. To my knowledge, this is the first published case study coauthored by professionals from both community and hospital facilities; as a result, it reminds us of the important role that hospitalization can play in an era of community-based treatment.

Finally, each of these case reports is followed by a commentary by a distinguished discussant with extensive clinical experience. The purpose of these commentaries is to initiate a dialogue about the following issues: In a field characterized by outreach and informality, what sort of professional boundaries in the case management relationship are required? When should case managers be assertive and when should they play a more passive role, allowing clients to set the pace of involvement? What sort of professional skills and training should case managers have? As case management values client empowerment and self-determination, are coercive interventions ever warranted and, if so, when and how should they be appropriately used? The intensely ideological dialogue on this issue has particularly stifled thoughtful reflection; by focusing on the reality of individual lives, we perhaps can examine the ethical conflicts and clinical challenges with greater care (Perlman, 1965; Will, 1968; Diamond and Wikler, 1985). Finally, when should case managers persist in their intervention strategies and when should they change gears and try another approach? All of these case studies reflect a degree of stubborn persistence—and even courage—on the part of their authors; when is this trait admirable and when does it interfere with experimenting with more useful approaches?

I invite the reader to join our dialogue in exploring these questions, discussing these issues with colleagues, supervisors, classmates, administrators, and consumers.

Joel Kanter
Editor

References

Diamond, R. J., and Wikler, D. I. "Ethical Problems in Community Treatment of the Chronically Mentally Ill." In L. I. Stein and M. A. Test (eds.), *The Training in Community Living Model: A Decade of Experience.* New Directions for Mental Health Services, no. 26. San Francisco: Jossey-Bass, 1985.

Harding, C. M., Brooks, G. W., Ashikago, T., Strauss, J. S., and Breier, A. "The Vermont Longitudinal Study of Persons with Severe Mental Illness, I: Methodology, Study Sample, and Overall Status 32 Years Later." *American Journal of Psychiatry,* 1987, *144,* 718–726.

Harding, C. M., and Strauss, J. S. "The Course of Schizophrenia: An Evolving Concept." In M. Alpert (ed.), *Controversies in Schizophrenia: Changes and Constancies.* New York: Guilford Press, 1985.

Harris, M., and Bergman, H. C. (eds.). *Case Management for Mentally Ill Patients: Theory and Practice.* Langhorne, Pa.: Harwood, 1993.

Kanter, J. S. "The Process of Change in the Chronic Mentally Ill: A Naturalistic Perspective." *Psychosocial Rehabilitation Journal,* 1985, *9* (1), 55–69.

Knee, R. I. *Better Social Services for Mentally Ill Patients: Proceedings of Institute on Social Work in Psychiatric Hospitals.* New York: American Association of Psychiatric Social Workers, 1955.

Perlman, H. H. "Self-Determination: Reality or Illusion?" *Social Service Review,* 1965, *39* (4), 410–421.

Schulz, C. G., and Kilgalen, R. K. *Case Studies in Schizophrenia.* New York: Basic Books, 1969.

Strauss, J. S., Hafez, H., Lieberman, P., and Harding, C. M. "The Course of Psychiatric Disorder, III: Longitudinal Principles." *American Journal of Psychiatry,* 1985, *142* (3), 289–296.

Will, O. A. "The Reluctant Patient, the Unwanted Psychotherapist—and Coercion." *Contemporary Psychoanalysis,* 1968, *5,* 1–31.

JOEL KANTER, M.S.W., L.C.S.W., is a senior case manager on the comprehensive support services unit of the Mount Vernon Center for Community Mental Health, Fairfax County, Virginia.

Case management has been part of the social work tradition for many years; this report of a creative, decade-long intervention with an isolated, older woman explores the boundaries between friendship and professional activity.

Casework as Friendship: A Long-Term Contact with a Paranoid Lady

Marjorie L. Sheppard
Commentary by Joel Kanter

The patient needs an experience, not an explanation.[1]

Mrs. X is nearly 72 at the time of writing. Just on ten years ago her husband was admitted to his district mental hospital as a voluntary patient with a depressive illness, and she was referred to me by the psychiatrist. She had disclosed to him quite severe paranoid delusions and it was felt she might need some help in her own right, although the main reason for referral was to try to divert anxiety from Mr. X both during his hospital stay and on his return home.

When I visited her at her home in central London, Mrs. X rather "shushed" me into the large bed-sitting-room and carefully locked the door before turning to speak to me. While she was then welcoming me in a friendly way and offering tea, I noted the room—beautifully kept and mainly occupied by an enormous double bed. Mrs. X was a spare woman of medium height, with dyed and "home" curled hair. Her face was lavishly made-up, suggesting not only a much younger woman but almost a prostitute. Her dress was well-cut and more modest, with a charming little scarf tucked in at the neck.

It was in speaking about her job during this first interview that her "delusions" showed themselves. She talked at great length about the "Man" who, she

This case study was previously published in the *British Journal of Psychiatric Social Work,* 1964, 7, 173–182. It is republished with the permission of the British Association of Social Workers.

said, was at the back of all her and her husband's troubles. For many years he had followed her everywhere and informed people about her because she refused to have sexual relations with him. He was now trying to force her into a situation where she would have to submit to his wishes: he had made her husband ill and unable to support her and was now interfering with her own capacity to keep a job and earn. He wanted any man—from young boy reaching puberty to old man approaching senility—to "have" her.

Mrs. X then explained the reason for her care in letting me in and for locking the door. The landlady was in league with the "Man," and the house (let out in rooms) was described as more or less a brothel. A young man (a relative of the landlady) who had a room on the top floor was particularly being urged to get Mrs. X to go to bed with him, and she was therefore at pains to avoid every possible contact with him. But she also locked the door against the landlady who, she said, would come in even when her husband was there and "pretend" to be asking after his health; but in fact, through the "Man," her object was to entice Mrs. X out of the room and upstairs into the young man's bed, so that she—the landlady—could "have" Mr. X. "But," said Mrs. X, "Mr. X hates anything like that just as much as I do."

Mrs. X said she thought the hospital was a "wonderful place," and appreciated the care and attention her husband was receiving from the doctors and nurses. She said how extraordinarily kind she felt it was of the psychiatrist to have asked me to call on her. It was agreed I should come again and continue to visit when her husband had returned home.

During these early visits Mrs. X talked freely for an hour or more, exhibiting great distress when speaking about the "Man." I had only seen Mr. X once in the hospital, and when he returned home a few weeks after admission I found him to be a gentle, quiet man; very deaf and often suffering severely from his "chest." Mrs. X spoke freely of the "Man" in front of him, and when she explained to him she had told me about their troubles he seemed to agree with her, joining in her "delusion."

It emerged that Mr. X had been a chauffeur in private service, and had met his wife in the course of duties; but what exactly she did or when or where they met was never disclosed. Nothing of her family background came to light except that she had no relatives. Mr. X, however, had wealthy relatives overseas, and the suggestion from Mrs. X was that he had not kept pace with them socially or materially. They had disapproved of his marriage to Mrs. X, but they sometimes wrote to him and allowed the couple a small weekly sum of money under his father's will. Up to Mr. X's recent admission to hospital he had worked daily, when his health permitted, for a private car hire firm for some time.

I continued to visit, and Mrs. X always plunged straight into talk about the "Man." Her husband was not really physically fit to take work, but when he tried for an occasional day's driving it was the "Man" who was getting in the way of his success: while the landlady was still being "encouraged" to get Mrs. X "upstairs." Meantime, Mr. X's chest pains—sometimes referred to as "indigestion"—got worse and worse. His wife described his agonies in the night, when she appeared to stay awake too and try to comfort him. During her talk about her husband, my impression grew that the couple had probably never either wanted or had intimate relations, that in some way they suited one another as if they were a homosexual pair; that they were all in all to one another in a loving, kindly, but non-physical, way, in their large double bed, and probably always had been. Only the "Man" was now trying to separate them by forcing them each to have an actual physical relationship with another person. On one or two occasions Mrs. X got very near to recounting details of some possible early indiscretion, and by asking a question at this moment I could probably have elicited her story; but I resisted any inclination to probe in this way. Sometimes she would say to me when she had been speaking about the "Man": "You do believe me, don't you?" And invariably I would reply: "Mrs. X, I know you yourself believe what you tell me to be so; it is outside my own experience, and I can only say I find it very strange but that I respect your belief." This would always seem to satisfy her.

Then, during the second year of my acquaintance with Mrs. X, her husband's "indigestion" proved to be cancer. He was admitted to the general hospital where I had my London office. Mrs. X visited him often, and she also then started to come to see me on the days I was there. She spoke of her husband always with a great feeling for him rather than for herself, as if she was part of him in his suffering and in his embarrassment during various physical examinations he had to undergo—"for he is a very modest man." During these weeks of anxiety she would often bring me tiny "posies" of flowers bought in the street, and would beg me at least occasionally to call on her at home, feeling that on her own she was at the greater mercy of the "Man." It was now that she began to use me literally as a moral support: she would say to me: "You look so good a person that if 'he' sees you are visiting me—coming into the house—he will not dare to try to have his way with me."

Before long Mr. X was sent to a Home for the Dying some distance away and I helped her with her fares. Finally, she phoned me that Mr. X had died. He been in great pain despite heavy sedation, and at the end scarcely knew her, but died in her arms.

With the question of funeral expenses, all her resentment about Mr. X's relatives came to the fore. She wanted her husband's body embalmed, and was angry when his relatives wrote they saw no reason to provide extra money for this, nor for a private grave. She spent the whole of his insurance money on the embalming, leaving only enough for the poorest coffin and funeral, and burial in a common grave. She asked me to go with her when she visited the embalmed body, which I did. She had only enough to buy a very small bouquet of flowers, and was glad when I told her I should like to give a similar bouquet, which was what she seemed to want. Ours were the only flowers on the coffin.

I realized Mrs. X would have no one to go with her to the funeral and asked if she would like me to accompany her. Another woman in the house had also offered to go and this had been agreed (this was the first time I had known Mrs. X accept any proffered outside friendship), and we both accompanied her. On the rather long journey to the outlying cemetery Mrs. X preserved a careful dignity not letting her grief show itself; but as the coffin was taken from the little chapel she went over to it and laid her head on it. Then—again for the first time—she took my arm and held on to me as we walked to the grave. She continued to hold my hand during the remainder of the ceremony and on the way home in the car. She talked of trying to get a room nearby and of planting bulbs on the grave.

Very shortly after this I visited Mrs. X at home and found her in bed. She was deluded and distraught, and I felt she was at the point of needing admission to a mental hospital. Indeed, she herself begged me to get her sent there, feeling that this was the one safe place where the "Man" could not harm her. Having spoken to her husband's psychiatrist, I telephoned the G.P. He had known Mrs. X for a long time and seemed surprised at my suggestion of mental hospital. She had never expressed her delusional ideas to him. He had prescribed for Mr. X from time to time, chiefly for a bronchial condition and difficulty in sleeping. As she certainly had a "bronchial condition" at the time the G.P. agreed to come to see her. She had pneumonia and he ordered an ambulance to take her to a general hospital at once. Her delusions were taken as part of a delirium, which perhaps they were at this time. Despite her state, Mrs. X was concerned that the room and she herself should be unkempt, and I helped her wash and comb her hair (and put on her lipstick) while we waited for the ambulance, and promised to return as soon as I could to tidy the room. I waited at the hospital with her while she was x-rayed and accompanied her on to the ward promising to visit her.

Perhaps stupidly I left my professional card behind, and when I did visit later Mrs. X said it had been thought she and not her husband had been the mental hospital patient and she had difficulty in getting the doctor to understand she had not intended to take her life with the sleeping tablets which were in her bag. She looked around to a corner at the head of the bed and said: "Mr. X is there, watching over me; he's glad I'm here and that you are my friend." There was no direct reference to the "Man" and she seemed to feel safe in the hospital where she had otherwise settled happily and quickly improved in physical health.

While in hospital, Mrs. X asked me to get one or two things from her room, not wanting her landlady to go through her belongings. During this visit for the first time I spoke with the landlady. She appeared to be an ordinary, decent sort of woman, quite understanding about Mrs. X's predicament. She certainly had no more idea of Mrs. X's delusions about the household than the G.P. and only described her as someone who tended to shut herself away and who did not respond in any way to friendly advances made by the landlady and others in the house. The landlady had been surprised Mrs. X had agreed to the woman accompanying us on the journey to the funeral. The husband was said to have been rather more friendly.

Somehow, up to this time, I had been uncertain in my own mind about whether there really was a legacy to come to Mrs. X. Then she asked me to help her again by going along to a city bank to inquire for any letters from abroad. I found she was quite well-known there, collecting letters from time to time. Mrs. X showed me the two I was given: one verified the fact of the legacy, making it quite clear (rather curtly) this was all she would get. The other was from Mr. X's relative, telling Mrs. X really to pull herself together; suggesting his family was very busy in one way or another and expected Mrs. X to be able to help herself and not to rely upon them for anything. I asked Mrs. X if she would like me to write to say she was ill, hoping the relatives might respond in a more sympathetic way. She welcomed this suggestion, but I had no reply to my letter, although after a time she herself received a letter more or less saying: "sorry you've been ill" and repeating how busy the family was. They sounded as if they lived in fair affluence.

Mrs. X had applied for her widow's pension and used her legacy to supplement it. She entertained me to an elaborate meal on her return home from hospital and later brought me a large bouquet of flowers to my office with a quite expensive present. She also sent a present to her husband's psychiatrist. She had always expressed a rather rueful feeling that this doctor did not like her personally and thought (like her relatives) she had not cared for her husband as well as she might have done: but through her gift she expressed her gratitude for the real help given to the one she had loved.

Mrs. X brought several more large bouquets to my office for me, and I was a little concerned at her fast spending of her modest legacy. I suggested that she might find out from the National Assistance Board at what point she could apply for assistance to supplement her pension, but she felt it was not right to do this until she had exhausted the legacy. Meantime, the landlady had slightly reduced her rent now she was living singly. Then she suggested to Mrs. X that the room was too big for her and wanted to put back the double bed she had replaced with a single one and let to a couple. With this, Mrs. X came to my office many times in a terrible state of anxiety. Each time she would twist herself round in her chair, looking away from me as she talked as if she was not fit for me to see or be with. Her face would screw up in misery and she would beat her hands in the air as she exclaimed: "He's making that young boy come after me: But I can't do it, I can't do it, I can't," her voice rising in a crescendo at the end. I felt at these times her agony of mind in myself, yet I only had to say quietly: "But of *course* you can't, Mrs. X; you are quite right not to go up to this young man's room." Then her body relaxed and, giving a relieved smile, she would say, "He knows he can't touch me while you are my friend." She would then ask me to go the house, if only occasionally. I did this.

During this period of strain she sometimes asked again about going to the mental hospital, and if they would not accept her as a patient if she could be employed there. I then asked her if she had ever considered going to an ordinary home for elderly people. I gave her the address of a voluntary organization which might assist her, and shortly after she took things entirely in her own hands, finding herself a reasonably priced "guest" house in a seaside town. I helped her arrange for some of her belongings to be put into store, and helped her safely out of her room and on to the train.

It was several months before we met again, but she wrote regularly to me. She did not write about the "Man," but was worried because there were men as well as women at the guest house. Then she wrote she was changing her residence. For a time she seemed to be happier, but the next I heard was that she was returning to London as the climatic conditions at the seaside town had caused a recurrence of her bronchitis.

Mrs. X found herself a furnished room in London, with a little kitchen attached. Here she once more entertained me to an elaborate meal—the last she provided for me—and made me a large cake to take home (she was an excellent cook). But once more on 'her own, she had been severely persecuted by the "Man," who she said was always hanging round the outside of the house and she feared might put a ladder to her window; or he was passing in some vehicle (she was living on a main street) and watching her. At this point she became physically ill again and was sent into another general hospital, where again she felt "safe." While there she spoke to me about getting a job as a resident cook/help and asked if I would act as a referee as to her honesty, etc. I agreed to this. As a result I was in touch with two elderly ladies who decided to engage her. Unfortunately, they "felt so sorry for" Mrs. X that they insisted upon trying to get her into company, introducing her to "suitable" people they felt might "cheer her up." It is possible she was somewhat extravagant in her housekeeping and "got up against" the employers because of this, but she left mainly because she could not bear the intrusion made upon her by the well-meaning attempts of the two ladies to socialize her. The employers subsequently wrote to me how "difficult" she had been, but their complaint was mainly that she did not "fit in" and they made no statement to suggest she had startled them by speaking of the "Man."

While she was in this job, Mrs. X's delusions returned very strongly; and when she was on the point of leaving she begged me to get her into a mental hospital. Indeed, I myself at that time again wondered if she might not be right. She had worked through her legacy and had nothing behind her except her pension. She now had no home and must once more seek a furnished room. However, I again spoke with her about the idea of going into an Old People's Home, perhaps a Council one, and she went of her own accord to County Hall and was admitted straight away to one of the very large institutional-type homes.

Mrs. X remained in this home for some considerable time, and I began to meet her for an occasional walk in the park followed by a cup of tea in a cafe. During this period she got very fat, probably through the starchy diet at the home. She lost her smart appearance, and gradually seemed to grow like the other straggly elderly people frequently met around the home. She would speak shudderingly of drunken women coming back into the large dormitory at night; of the difficulties of washing with others looking on (often she rose very early to avoid this); of being forced to bathe with an attendant present; and most of all of the old men with whom she had to mix at meals and in the sitting-rooms. Sometimes we met these men when out walking together, and she would hold tightly on to my arm and yet at the same time I could feel she made some kind of movement toward them. Behind each one of them she saw the "Man."

Mrs. X pointed out the hopelessness of it all. She might as well be dead. "He" would never let her be. Her very fatness at this time was a horror to her, and while she could not afford a corset she clutched her (fortunately volumi-nous) coat around her so that no one could see her figure. She constantly referred to the lines on her face and how dreadful she looked, although she still made up her face and endeavored, for example by wearing a small chiffon scarf at her neck, to achieve some smartness. I asked her if she would like me to try to help her toward a transfer to one of the Council's smaller homes, although I began to doubt if she would be considered suitable. However, a favorable reply was received to my application and her name was placed on the waiting list. Meantime I helped her buy a corset and also began occasion-ally to take her out to lunch to offset the pretty dull diet at the home. In the restaurant she tried to hide away, referring to her "awful" appearance.

The wait for transfer to another home went on for a year or more, the delay being partly because Mrs. X so badly wanted to be near her husband's grave. Meantime, although she still spoke freely of the "Man," she seemed to be making an occasional friendship with one or two of the more "respectable" women at the home, being particularly drawn to one who had once been in the same mental hospital as her husband. These friendships were not at all close, but involved recommending books to one another and discussing what they read. Mostly these were novels strongly tinged with reference to the phys-ical act of sex, which she could speak about to me without sign of disturbance. In other ways she remained on her own: walking in the park even in the colder weather or sitting reading in the enormous dayroom at the home, which I had visited and where I had observed the easy isolation possible within the crowd. She still longed for a job and felt herself capable of work: but when we dis-cussed this might mean the loss of her place on the waiting list for the small home, she decided against it. Meantime, she felt unable to assist with domes-tic chores at the home, valuing her freedom to get out of it more than the small amount of pocket money she would receive thereby. She still worried about her clothes, but did not want the box of things she had in store to be sent to her for fear of losing what she did possess.

Then, quite suddenly, she was offered a place in a small voluntary home and had to make an immediate decision about taking this. It was not near her husband's grave, but she decided she had better go in case she "upset the authorities" (always her fear). I visited her at this home, and she took me round and introduced me to the matron and one or two other residents. She liked the matron and had already become involved in doing many jobs, being one of the youngest and most active. She once more became smarter in appearance, fairly quickly getting thinner again and at the same time happier in her looks. She now had her box, and had also been supplied by the Council with some other fairly nice clothing. She was delighted she had a little room to herself. The meals were more daintily served and of greater variety. Her one worry, however, was that there were still three or four old men residents. She had so hoped to be with women only, although by her talk with me she had obviously sometimes spoken with the men of her own accord.

While in this home she had another spell in a general hospital with bronchial trouble, and she also had great difficulty in sleeping. This occurred following a change of matron, and when at the same time the food became less good. While in hospital she said she wanted to go back to the large institution, but eventually returned to the small home where she continued to help with domestic chores although she did not join in any group activities. She spoke less and less of the "Man," however, although at times of crisis "he" was brought up as the cause of the trouble.

Now (since about four years ago) began our fairly regular bi-monthly or three monthly meetings for lunch. After a bit, these took place on a Saturday, with a cinema and tea before she departed home. This arose because she now lived on the far side of London from my own home and office, and later on the plan was reinforced when I changed my job and could no longer ask her to my office. She still wanted to be able to get to her husband's grave more frequently, and both of us had continued to press for exchange to another home because of this. Eventually, some three years ago, she was offered a place in another voluntary home and she accepted this although not quite happy because it was not directly under the Council and it was still "mixed." It also meant sharing a room with one other lady, which at first proved hard as the other occupant (whom I met and noted to be very dominating) had taken the best part of the room and hardly ever left it. However, Mrs. X solved this problem by going out a great deal, as well as discovering that in this home no one except herself seemed to want to use the special TV room. In TV she has found much solace in the evenings and what she sees now often provides topics for conversation when we meet.

Over the last three years, the "Man" has only been mentioned once, and I almost began to think I must have "imagined" him—she was in all other ways such a perfectly ordinary, normal woman. She continued to take pride in her appearance, and somehow her heavy make-up suited her as did the smart little hats (often picked up in a jumble sale and altered by her) and clothing she had given her occasionally, of good quality and cut. She seemed to gain overall confidence in herself. We now lunched in a fairly good type of restaurant, and she no longer tried to hide from the gaze of others; indeed she would speak in a friendly way with the waiter or any other customer—man or woman—who might also sit at our table.

On the one occasion the "Man" did return, just over a year ago, Mrs. X telephoned me at my home. She said she was "in great trouble" but that she could not say over the telephone what the trouble was: could I possibly meet her soon. Over a meal two days later she told me she had been asked to do some task at the home which, when described, I personally felt a job for staff and a bit much to ask an elderly resident to undertake. She had told the chairman of the committee she felt she could not do it but had been taken to task over the matter. She was terrified of getting into the black books of the committee if she stuck out against them. Not having spoken of the "Man" for so long, she suddenly said to me: "He's behind it, you know: he's still there: you know that, don't you. He'll never leave me alone." I told her (as I had told her about the sexual problem): "I agree with you, Mrs. X. This is not a job for you; I think you are perfectly justified to tell the chairman you don't feel able to undertake it." The same sigh of relief occurred. She subsequently acted upon my suggestion, and as far as I could gather later on, although some disappointment was expressed in her, nothing further has been said about the matter and no more onerous tasks have been asked of her.

Apart from this incident, there has been no sign of disturbance. The "difficult" lady who shared Mrs. X's room has now been sent elsewhere and Mrs. X has a companion with whom she is on reasonable terms. Her only complaint about the home is that the meals are so small and that she, unlike most of the other residents who have relatives to bring them eatables and provide extra pocket money, gets very hungry. When we meet, we now have a "slap-up" lunch, of which she eats every bit with the utmost enjoyment, while she compares the quantity of each item with that provided at the home. She apparently talks to the other residents of her lunches with me and what we do on these days out, in order, I feel, to let it be known she too has a friend.

Somehow recently Mrs. X's pleasure in these meetings has communicated itself to me, so that I myself really look forward to them and enjoy the meal as much as she does. Earlier on she gave to me: first the tea, then the meals at her home, then the flowers and gifts according to her income. Now I give to her. We both know she can no longer give to me, although from time to time she will bring a tiny bunch of flowers or small token. At first she received my gifts to her with worry and a shamed looking away; but now she can take, and when I leave her nowadays she kisses me on the cheek, as if I was a younger relative, while I return her kiss.

In the cinema I have usually found she enjoys a film where there is, if not a "happy family," the presentation of the older man (husband/father) who cares for his wife and children and who protects them from what might be felt to be illicit advances from the "bad" man. It so happened we first lighted upon one or two such films, and I tend now to try to choose a Saturday for our meeting when such a film is showing. During the performance and after, Mrs. X will seem happy and often say: "He was such a nice man, so good." On one more recent occasion, too, where the "bad" man displayed some good qualities she was able to appreciate and refer to this.

Mrs. X, the last time I saw her, asked me how she might join some organization where she could meet people outside the home, and we discussed the possibility of her going to a women's guild, or some of the day classes available.

She now goes on any outings from the home (although earlier she avoided these), and shops for the more infirm residents.

Discussion

Mrs. X perhaps represents a common enough case to the community and mental hospital social worker. She is one of the many late middle-aged and elderly women of good personality and capacity who has a well-systematized "delusion" in one direction, often of a sexual nature. Why have I chosen to tell her story? First, I think, to examine why she did not get into hospital; second, to examine the way in which support in the community can perhaps be achieved to the patient's advantage without probing, but simply by offering some security within a friendship.

In thinking about why Mrs. X has not got into a mental hospital, I am reminded of some other cases I have known: The woman who shouted at the "ghosts" who came through the walls of her room and called her a "bad woman"; another who called out to the little gnomes sitting on her bed at night, who tweaked her limbs and expostulated with her for some mild "sin"; a third who was tormented by a red-headed man and who banged on the floor of her room trying to stop him passing electric currents through her body.

These and others I encountered after they had disturbed their neighbors and been brought into hospital. Once in hospital the usual practice is to want to know the background history, while the patient is periodically and relentlessly prodded and questioned to find out if the "delusion" is still there; and often if someone manages to drag out the "delusion" everyone is very pleased. This would seem to lead either to a continuation of the delusional idea in this type of patient (even an increase or development); or else he learns not to speak of his "delusions" in order to get out of hospital. He may be followed up for a time, but perhaps is "dropped" if he seems fairly free of his "delusions" and is left alone until the bottled up anxiety (expressed in the "delusion" as other patients express anxiety in some psychosomatic illness—Mrs. X did both) leads to the "delusion" emerging again with further resulting trouble with neighbors and possible readmission to the hospital. Few people want to listen to the "delusions" so that the patient, no longer able to keep them within himself, is now forced to speak of them to more people. He becomes "well-known," and he is quickly aware even the sympathetic listener doubts the truth of what he is saying and constantly tries to persuade him that to exist in the community he must recognize "it is all in his imagination." He therefore feels too insecure to exist in the community.

It has seemed to me that Mrs. X could on a number of occasions have got into a mental hospital and have become a "known" person in this way. This could possibly have stood in the way of her fairly easy admission to a small old people's home where she is now a useful member of the community. I think the reason why her story went this way lies in the fact of her early discovery and referral to me, so that I was able to become her friend and support through the various crises in her immediate life history as they occurred—when her husband was first admitted to a mental hospital; then when he went into hospital with cancer; when he died; when she lost her home and job; when she was physically ill and admitted to a general hospital; when she was without money; when she was neglected and ashamed.

I am sure that her husband was a companion and support without which she could not exist. Someone was needed to take his place, and this was necessary in his lifetime because she sensed his impending death. He was her "protector." I came from an institution (an "authority") which had housed him she felt with care and lovingness, and I was early on invested with these qualities myself. He was the "good" man: I was the "good" woman. I became Mrs. X's "moral support" (one might say her "guardian angel") who warded off evil from her. When dead, her husband at times became very vividly present to her and approved of what she was with me. I could if necessary guide her into some kind of institution of a protective nature, and help her to keep on good terms with those in authority there.

At the same time, I "approved" of her sticking up for her rights, and the fact that I saw no reason for her to enter the mental hospital when she wished to do this signified I upheld her sanity. I did not probe into her history; in fact I still do not know her background history. Although I did not actually enter into her "delusion," I respected it and told her so; that is, I recognized that to her it was real—who was I to question its truth? This was something she was experiencing and I was not. That was all. When the child wakes from a nightmare in terror and still has the events in mind, the mother cannot always explain the fear or understand it; but she can experience the terror with him by being with him in his moment of fear. A truly shared terrifying experience in this way sometimes loses its terror.

My attitude meant that Mrs. X could always come to me immediately when any anxiety brought back the "delusion" instead of holding on to it in a way which might have led to its development.

How did I come to work in this way and to adopt this attitude? I started without any preconceived ideas, and it is perhaps on looking back that certain things stand out. From the beginning, because of her age, I felt it would be wrong to risk breaking down Mrs. X by questioning her about the origin of her delusions. Although I was tempted at times to find out "why," there appeared to me no real reason for this other than my own curiosity and wish to tie things up into a "case." When my own temporary anxieties nearly led me to press for her admission to a mental hospital and this proved unnecessary, I slowly became convinced of Mrs. X's own capacity to keep integrated provided she had me as the friend she wanted. She still refers to me in letters and verbally as "my very good friend," and it seemed very important to her to look upon me in this light.

I had to be a friend, but also a "good" friend; because the other important thing was that my "goodness" could help to defeat the badness in the "Man" and thereby save Mrs. X from being harmed. It was really quite intuitively at first that I used these two tools put into my hands by Mrs. X herself. As time went on I think some of my "goodness" entered into Mrs. X, and that this was later supplemented by the films which verified for her there were "good" men also. There was no need for interpretation from me.

Perhaps one of the most valuable tools the social worker has ever had is that her position allows her to sit down with her "client" in a friendly way, or as person to person. Recently the patient undergoing treatment in the general hospital has been voicing very much the feeling that he is treated as a "thing"; his body is examined to discover why it is not working properly and then something is "done to" his body to put it right, but he "himself" is overlooked. Similarly, I believe that where there is too much involvement with the mechanics of the mind in treating the mental patient, when we are *too* busy thinking and asking questions (both of ourselves and patient) while we are with him, the person—the human being—tends to be forgotten. This attitude communicates itself to the patient and something in the relationship is lost.

It is not denied that the worker needs to be aware of the possible underlying reasons for the patient's behavior and for her own, but is she not perhaps sometimes being diverted from her true function as a "support" and friend to the patient and relative into the expert who needs must interpret to him? There is, I think, a tendency amongst more highly trained caseworkers to consider that the "friendly relationship" way of working with the client is an inferior way. This seems a pity, as apart from the lack of highly trained workers who can offer interpretative casework help to all who might benefit by it, there are many cases where it is neither wise nor necessary to do so, any more than it is possible or useful to offer analysis or analytic psychotherapy to all patients.

A professional casework relationship is considered to differ from a friendship in that in friendship two people each expect to receive from and give to the other, whereas in the professional relationship the first consideration is to the client. Yet most of us probably have amongst our personal friends one who gives more to us than we to him and one to whom we give more. But we still consider this person our friend. I think we can extend this sort of friendship to certain clients. The difference is perhaps that, while we permit ourselves a similar involvement in the sense of allowing ourselves to feel liking or love for the client and are able to receive from him as well as to give to him, we do retain a certain professional distance: but only in the sense that we do not "demand" anything of the client or feel we have a "right" to return of affection or reciprocal behavior which we might still expect from our other friends.

Although this way of working could, I suggest, be used more often than it is by the skilled caseworker, I also believe that many less highly trained workers could use it profitably. It implies an understanding of two of the basic principles taught in the very beginnings of social work training—and often the hardest to learn—that you need to "listen" and to "empathize." You then really "sit back and let things roll over you." You are not worried about your position vis-à-vis the client in the sense that you are a "worker," and you are not worried about "what things mean" any more than you are likely to be in your relationship with a personal friend. While listening, you convey to your client that here is another human being like yourself. In this situation, the freedom of feeling which lies between yourself and the client is, I believe, beneficial in itself. Also, more frequently than may be thought, the client will interpret for himself if we "let him be" in this way.

The skill of the highly-trained caseworker could perhaps be utilized more often than it is in discerning which kind of case needs which kind of approach, rather than, having acquired a high skill in this, using the interpretative technique in all instances. There is not just the need to assess the client's capacity to understand interpretation, but to consider if this is helpful or advisable in a given situation. I am sure Mrs. X had the capacity to understand interpretation, but I am equally sure such an approach would have disturbed her unnecessarily, and that sometimes the more roundabout route is a shorter one in the long-run. In much community work where it is important that the client should not break down, and with the older person who is less likely to be able to "alter," the important and truly healing things seem to me to be through the actual relationship or growing "love" of the existing person. With Mrs. X the continued support led to an ability to "stay put" rather than to alter. Although no insight has perhaps been gained, because anxiety has been less and someone "good" was always available, the "delusion" (the anxiety symptom) has receded and at times been lost.

While writing up this story of Mrs. X, I was reading an essay by Rollo May (1961) and the following quotes put far more clearly than I can what I have in mind:

> I have, for a number of years, been struck, as a practicing therapist and teacher of therapists, how often our concern with trying to understand the patient in terms of the mechanisms by which his behavior takes place blocks our understanding of what he really is experiencing . . . if, as I sit here, I am chiefly thinking of these *whys* and *hows* of the way the problem came about, I will have grasped everything *except the most important thing of all, the existing person.* Indeed, I will have grasped everything except the only source of data I have, namely, this experiencing human being, this person now emerging, becoming . . . immediately in the room with me.

Note

1. A remark made personally to Rollo May by Frieda Fromm-Reichmann.

Reference

May, R. "The Emergence of Existential Psychology." In R. May (ed.), *Existential Psychology.* New York: Random House, 1961.

MARJORIE L. SHEPPARD was head social worker at St. Bernard's Hospital in London, England.

Commentary

Joel Kanter, M.S.W., L.C.S.W.
Senior Case Manager
Mount Vernon Center for Community Mental Health

When I first came across Marjorie Sheppard's case report "Casework as Friendship: A Long-Term Contact With a Paranoid Lady," I was immediately impressed with her caring, commitment, and clinical acumen in working with an older, isolated woman who totally rejected the patient, or even client, role. Working patiently and persistently over a decade in a manner that we would now identify as "case management," Sheppard assists Mrs. X, without the use of antipsychotic medications, in finding stable and rewarding residential arrangements, developing new social relationships, and in ameliorating severe schizoid and paranoid personality characteristics that had greatly handicapped her. In the process, Sheppard engages in a variety of activities that would be considered boundary violations according to current psychiatric norms, including giving and receiving gifts and taking Mrs. X to lunch and movies outside of her regular working hours (Gutheil and Gabbard, 1993).

Beyond the mere reporting of her work with Mrs. X, however, Sheppard challenges us intellectually, exploring whether the essential elements in her relationship with Mrs. X were anything more than what occurs in friendship. This is a critical question for the case management field. If the answer to this question is affirmative, then we should seriously consider Sheppard's suggestion that "less highly trained workers" be used to provide such services. At the same time, her report also challenges the goal-directed treatment planning found in almost all case management programs. Sheppard never formulates goals with Mrs. X and instead views her own listening and empathy as the central "therapeutic" ingredients. Although Sheppard helps Mrs. X obtain environmental resources, these interventions were more often a response to crises than part of a case management plan. In this commentary, I will explore these issues in more detail.

To have a fuller appreciation of Sheppard's case report, it is helpful to have more knowledge of her professional life. Although I have been unable to locate anyone in England who knew her well or worked directly with her, I have been able to learn that she "qualified" as a psychiatric social worker (roughly equivalent to an M.S.W.) at St. Clement's Hospital in 1952. Later, she worked at Horton Hospital and was the head social worker at St. Bernard's Hospital in London in 1966. (Personnel records at this hospital were destroyed in a fire.)

Besides this paper, Sheppard published three other articles, one on group therapy with schizophrenic patients (1960), one on family intervention (1963), and one that discussed how social workers integrate environmental and psychological interventions (1966). Although the case report in this volume only contained one reference to the professional literature, her other articles have many more citations and suggest that she was quite familiar with the emerging literature on the individual and family therapy of schizophrenia as well as with George Brown's early research on family expressed emotion. Sheppard's 1963 paper on family intervention is an astute precursor of the family psychoeducation movement as she identifies the limitations of "family blaming" and discusses how to collaborate with relatives to reduce stress in the home. Similarly, her 1966 article on "material and practical aid" is an excellent discussion of the psychological importance of environmental assistance in helping very disturbed clients.

These writings clearly indicate that Sheppard was an extremely well educated and skilled social worker and that her work with Mrs. X was certainly informed by this clinical training and experience. This conceptual underpinning was evident in her case report as she demonstrated a sophisticated understanding of delusional symptoms, the role of empathy in the therapeutic process, the use of splitting by paranoid individuals (that is, "goodness" and "badness"), and the unintended consequences of the patient role.

In my opinion, it is highly unlikely that Sheppard would have been able to function as she did with Mrs. X without this professional skill, though paradoxically this very skill enabled her to avoid a conventionally "professional" treatment strategy that would have either derailed the engagement process or effectively socialized Mrs. X into a passive, and likely institutional, patient role. Because she understood the dynamics of Mrs. X's disorder, Sheppard was able to tolerate the countertransference anxiety evoked by Mrs. X's paranoia and the ambiguity of their "social worker–client" relationship (Kanter, 1988). Obviously, Mrs. X's eccentricities and isolative behavior did not evoke caretaking or friendly responses by sources of natural support in her community or family; only one other person even attended her husband's funeral.

I think it is highly likely that if today's case managers met Mrs. X, they would decide that she was "in denial" of her illness, perhaps try to educate her about schizophrenia and its psychopharmacological treatment, and even seek to have her involuntarily hospitalized. In terms of her residential needs, efforts would be made to link her to residential programs for the mentally ill, programs that likely would reject her because she was not cooperative with psychiatric treatment. Alternatively, some assertive outreach programs might have inadvertently evoked her paranoid defenses by visiting too often and attempting to place her in appropriate housing.

Instead, Sheppard wisely allows Mrs. X to control the level of involvement in their relationship. At times, they meet frequently in Sheppard's office; at other times, they meet sporadically in restaurants or at Mrs. X's residence. But for the most part, Sheppard's interventions were not assertive.

Over time, Mrs. X's "recovery" from a paranoid disorder may have been a spontaneous recovery in which Sheppard's main role was to avoid linking Mrs. X with psychiatric and institutional settings that might have arrested these changes. More likely, though, Sheppard played a catalytic role (Bennett, 1989), making herself available in a crisis situation (the death of Mr. X) and assisting over time in a reparative mourning process. In this process, Mrs. X identified with Sheppard's integrative ego capacities (Harris and Bergman, 1987), largely relinquished her paranoid defenses, especially splitting and projection, and as she viewed others more realistically, began to develop a capacity for more fulfilling relationships.

This process, however, was a slow one and required a long-term commitment by Sheppard. Unfortunately, the low pay and status of case managers does not encourage them to establish a career with a particular program or agency. In many case management programs, an "experienced" case manager is a worker with two years' experience. Although I agree with Sheppard that a paraprofessional worker could have achieved a similar outcome, especially with supervision, it is unlikely that anyone with the combination of empathy, judgment, intelligence, and persistence that Mrs. X required would continue in a case management system with the current levels of stresses and rewards.

Sheppard also highlights one of the major dilemmas of using paraprofessionals in this work: that it requires skills in empathic listening—"to sit back and let things roll over you"—that are "often the hardest to learn." Unfortunately, as training in psychotherapy has become devalued, case managers with professional backgrounds often have no more of these skills than their paraprofessional colleagues. In many settings, case managers are taught to respond to psychotic symptoms by making a prompt referral for psychiatric consultation or renegotiating the treatment plan; they have received no training at all in techniques of psychotherapeutic management that might be more efficacious (Weiden and Havens, 1994).

Finally, the central question raised by this paper is whether casework or case management is, or should be, more than a type of friendship. As Sheppard comments, there are many social relationships that are not fully reciprocal: friendships frequently develop where one person "looks out for" another. Atkinson (1986) suggests that perhaps half of all persons with severe mental illness have such a "competent other."

However, while these friends, family members, neighbors, and volunteers provide valuable assistance, their support is clearly inadequate for the majority of individuals with severe mental illness. When case managers attempt to meet these needs, a caring, friendly demeanor is certainly an essential attitude, and relationships often develop where clients view their case managers as their best friends. For various reasons, though, including their own needs for personal support, case managers cannot and should not see clients as *their* friends; regardless of the informality of the contact, they must maintain an ongoing sensitivity to their clients' needs and well-being and place these above their own. This responsibility, so exemplified by Sheppard, is ultimately what differentiates case management from friendship, enabling us as case managers to persist in our efforts even when there is little response to our own needs. Yet, within these parameters, there are still many opportunities for a rich and fulfilling interaction that enhances the humanity of both clients and case managers.

Commentary References

Atkinson, D. "Engaging Competent Others: A Study of the Support Networks of People with Mental Handicap." *British Journal of Social Work,* 1986, *16* (suppl.), 83–101.

Bennett, M. J. "The Catalytic Function in Psychotherapy." *Psychiatry,* 1989, *52,* 351–364.

Gutheil, T. G., and Gabbard, G. O. "The Concept of Boundaries in Clinical Practice: Theoretical and Risk-Management Dimensions." *American Journal of Psychiatry,* 1993, *150* (2), 188–196.

Harris, M., and Bergman, H. C. "Case Management with the Chronically Mentally Ill: A Clinical Perspective." *American Journal of Orthopsychiatry,* 1987, *57* (2), 296–302.

Kanter, J. S. "Clinical Issues in the Case Management Relationship." In M. Harris and L. Bachrach (eds.), *Clinical Case Management.* New Directions for Mental Health Services, no. 40. San Francisco: Jossey-Bass, 1988.

Sheppard, M. L. "Psychotherapy with a Small Group of Chronic Schizophrenic Patients." *British Journal of Psychiatric Social Work,* 1960, 5 (3), 4–12.

Sheppard, M. L. "Some Reflections on Work with the Schizophrenic and His Family." *British Journal of Psychiatric Social Work,* 1963, 7 (1), 13–20.

Sheppard, M. L. "The Social Worker's Use of Material and Practical Aid." *British Journal of Psychiatric Social Work,* 1966, 8 (3), 28–34.

Weiden, P., and Havens, L. "Psychotherapeutic Management Techniques in the Treatment of Outpatients with Schizophrenia." *Hospital and Community Psychiatry,* 1994, *45,* 549–555.

A supportive family and case manager collaborate to help a reclusive, schizophrenic woman to emerge from psychosis and create a fulfilling life.

Terri: Family-Centered Case Management

Joel Kanter
Commentary by Kayla F. Bernheim

This case report describes five and a half years of work with Terri B. (a young, African-American, treatment-resistant, schizophrenic female) and her parents. Throughout most of the time I have known her, Terri has lived in her parental home and the case management was largely a collaborative process between her parents and myself. Although Terri eventually became involved in a variety of other treatments and services, including psychopharmacology, supportive psychotherapy, psychosocial rehabilitation, and residential treatment, the family intervention was essential to engaging her in these other modalities that cumulatively have resulted in a positive outcome.

Both Mr. and Mrs. B. are successful, well-educated professionals; Terri's father has a Ph.D., and her mother has an M.A. Terri's childhood as the oldest of three siblings was unremarkable; she did well in a competitive public school system, was a member of a school athletic team and had a number of girlfriends. However, there is some indication that she tended in high school to associate more with a group of friends than to develop close friendships.

Some identity conflicts became apparent in college, where Terri started at a nearby large public university, transferred after one year to a smaller black college, and transferred again for her last two years to a prestigious private institution near her parents' home. Although both of these transfers were motivated by a desire to find a social milieu where she would feel comfortable, she felt estranged from the social life of all of these schools, even though she always lived in the dormitories and became acquainted with many students.

After graduation, Terri obtained an entry-level professional job in her field of study and lived in her own apartment about ten miles away from her parents. Over the next several years, she continued to do poorly in her social relationships, changing jobs several times and becoming increasingly reclusive when she was not at work. Finally, she lost her job and it became apparent to Mr. and Mrs. B. that she had become quite paranoid, rarely leaving her apartment or answering the phone. They made an unsuccessful attempt to commit Terri to a hospital before bringing her home to live with them.

Over the next eighteen months, Terri was totally isolated and refused all treatment or social contact. She spent almost all her time staring at TV in her room, coming down to the kitchen briefly to fix herself meals. She exhibited no psychotic ideation but refused to communicate on any level. She engaged in compulsive activities in the bathroom that consumed two rolls of toilet paper daily. Because she was not a danger to herself or others, she was not committable. At this point in time, Mr. and Mrs. B. contacted me to help them engage Terri in treatment and assist her restoring her functioning.

Year One

I hold one two-hour meeting in my office to review history from parents and develop a relationship. A week later, I visit the home to try to speak with Terri. She is lying on her bed staring at TV in a neat, undecorated room. She does not respond to my questions beyond suggesting that I am interfering with her television viewing. She appears affectless and switches channels without any particular interest in what she is watching. I depart after twenty minutes. I return two weeks later for another home visit with the same result. I meet again with her parents in my office and review my observations. I suggest that they monitor any changes closely and stay in contact with me; if there is some deterioration, we may be able to arrange for her hospitalization. Over the next few months, I stay in monthly phone contact with Mrs. B., who reports no change in her daughter's condition.

Five Months. Mrs. B. calls to report that Terri has become extremely agitated; she is running around the house nude, making lewd and threatening remarks. I arrange an emergency home visit within hours. When I arrive, she is upstairs, still nude, and is yelling obscenities. She is clearly upset about my presence ("get that [expletive] out of here"), and I make no attempt to go upstairs. I advise Mr. and Mrs. B. to immediately go to the judge to obtain a detention order. Terri is detained within hours and sent to the state hospital.

On the Tuesday after Labor Day, Mrs. B. calls me to report that the hospital social worker has asked her to pick up Terri today. Because of the Labor Day weekend, the family was not notified of the hearing today, so Terri was released on a technicality after five days in the hospital. She has refused all medication, and she has returned to her previous uncommunicative state. I recommend an emergency family meeting on their return home from the hospital. I advise the parents to state that they will not take Terri home unless she agrees to cooperate with an outpatient psychiatric assessment, attend biweekly family sessions, and perform some minimal chores. If she refuses to do this, they should put her in a motel while negotiations continue.

In our meeting, they implement this plan. Terri becomes irate and insists on returning home without conditions. The parents hold their ground, and I pick up the phone several times to call the motel. Finally, after ninety minutes, Terri agrees to comply with her parents' conditions, and the family returns home.

Four days later, another family session is held. I take a social history from Terri in her parents' presence. Although her affect is flat and she exhibits little insight, she does cooperate to the extent of giving me basic information about her educational and employment history. She offers little, however, about the development of her illness and denies any difficulties. I refer her to a female psychiatrist for an extended evaluation.

Over the next six months, Terri and her parents continue to attend biweekly family sessions on a regular basis. Terri has little to contribute and I spend much of the meetings chatting casually with her parents. Terri denies that she has any difficulties and defends her current functioning as a chosen lifestyle. We do discuss several issues including her progress in the extended psychiatric evaluation. The psychiatrist is trying to develop a therapeutic alliance, and the evaluation is extended over several months. The psychiatrist refers Terri to her internist and a neurologist for further evaluation, but their findings are largely negative. The psychiatrist is not able to achieve any consensus with Terri about her difficulties and concludes her meetings in several months. As Terri was unwilling to take any medications, even iron pills for anemia, psychotropic medications could not be considered.

In our family meetings, we also discuss her excessive use of toilet paper but are unable to achieve a consensus. At the end of each session, I meet privately with Mr. and Mrs. B. for about ten minutes; Terri does not seem to mind this and seems relieved to be able to leave the office. In these parental contacts, they agree to begin to give Terri a $10/week allowance; predictably, she initially rejects this money but eventually begins to squirrel it away and then spends it. She had not been in a commercial establishment in two years.

In our third family meeting (held around noon), I terminate the session early and ask the family to come with me to an Italian deli around the corner, where I buy Terri a slice of their unique homemade pizza. She seems pleased by this, and at the next session, we go on a similar expedition to a nearby Jamaican lunch spot. In a phone call to Mrs. B. between meetings, I recommend that the parents stop for lunch at a restaurant after our next session. Terri accompanies them for a seated meal without comment. The biweekly meetings become an occasion for family outings, and Terri begins to use her funds to shop. They also see several movies and go bowling.

Ten Months. Terri is taking some walks during the week in her neighborhood to a nearby convenience store. However, her demeanor in our sessions remains unchanged and she still spends most of her time alone in her room. For several weeks, she becomes interested in crocheting, but soon becomes frustrated with this.

Year Two

Terri asks her mother to buy paint to redecorate her room. She completes the project with minimal help. She also asks her parents to take her for a day trip to a regional amusement park. Surprised by this request, they agree and have a pleasant trip. In our continuing biweekly sessions, an invitation to a June wedding of Terri's high school friend is discussed. Although she refused to make a decision until the last minute, Terri accompanies her parents on a 200-mile trip to her friend's wedding, but stays in the motel during the ceremony and reception. She does go on with them to spend several days at the beach and participates in recreational activities.

Sixteen Months. In a family meeting, Terri expresses an interest in employment for the first time. She says she would like to work as a salesperson in the women's clothing department of an upscale store. Though rational, her speech sounds somewhat pressured. Later that evening, Mrs. B. calls me to report that Terri has decompensated. Mr. B. obtains another detention petition, and Terri is rehospitalized at the state hospital.

Three weeks after admission, Mrs. B. reports that the hospital plans to discharge Terri the next day because she refuses to take medication. A family meeting is scheduled before discharge. Consulting with Mrs. B. and the hospital social worker, I recommend that her parents tell Terri that she cannot return home unless she takes medication. (This will also stop the discharge plans as the hospital is reluctant to discharge patients without a home.) Without any fanfare, Terri immediately agrees to begin medications in the family session, and she is retained at the hospital.

I work with the hospital staff by telephone to reformulate discharge plans. Terri takes a hospital bus to begin to attend a psychosocial day program one day a week, and I meet her there for her application interview for this program. I advocate with their intake coordinator to ignore her poor functioning in recent months and place her in the more vocational units of their program. I also arrange for her to begin outpatient treatment with a second female psychiatrist, involving medications and biweekly supportive psychotherapy sessions.

After Terri's discharge, we resume our biweekly family meetings. Terri attends the day program regularly but expresses little interest in other members or the activities. However, neuroleptic medication seems to have a significant impact on the quantity and quality of her communications, and her parents report more spontaneous conversations.

Eighteen Months. Terri continues to attend the day program regularly for several months. She gets a paid position ringing bells for the Salvation Army but quits this after several days; subsequently, her attendance at the day program declines. She claims that the program is not interesting to her, but she is not interested in any other activity. Within a month, she stops attending the program and makes sporadic attempts to look for work.

About a month after leaving the day program, Terri obtains a part-time position doing clerical work for a businesswoman in her home. While it sounded ideal in terms of reasonable hours and a personal work environment, Terri is uncertain she is doing good work and quits after several weeks. Soon after, she discontinues her medications, claiming that she does not think they are helping her. However, she continues to meet with her psychiatrist. Recognizing Terri's impressive willfulness, the psychiatrist, her parents, and I decide not to try to persuade her to resume her medications. To do so would likely provoke a battle of wills and would be unlikely to achieve the desired outcome.

Within a month, Terri reports feeling "depressed"; her psychiatrist and I are uncertain what she means by this, but she agrees to a trial of antidepressant medications. Several weeks later, she agrees to resume her neuroleptic medication. She works a few days for a temporary agency but does not like this. I discover that she began receiving Social Security Disability (SSDI) benefits several months earlier as a result of an application made at the state hospital.

Year Three

After expressing little interest in structured activities for several months in the biweekly family sessions, Terri obtains a volunteer clerical position at an agency for mentally retarded persons. Within a month, her hours increase from twelve to twenty-five weekly and she is given increasing responsibility as the staff are impressed with her skills and reliability. She is offered a paid position with the agency, but she expresses considerable anxiety about this change. Although it does not appear to involve any change in her hours or duties, she is troubled by the symbolic change.

Soon after, her psychiatrist takes a five-week vacation to get married. Although Terri had never expressed any special attachment or affection for her, she abruptly terminates her volunteer job and medication soon after her psychiatrist's departure. I advise her parents to avoid overreacting when Terri says she never wants to work or take medication again.

Thirty Months. Terri resumes her medication several weeks after her psychiatrist returns. A month later, she expresses an interest in the family meetings to move from her parents' home to a supervised apartment program. When I inform her that all of these programs will require that she be involved in a structured day activity, she initiates an investigation (with my urging) into all of the local alternatives. After contacting several programs, she decides to enroll in a hospital-based day treatment program with an intensive psychotherapeutic focus. While initially noncommunicative in the group therapy sessions, she seems interested in the problems of other members. I consult with the day program staff to discuss how they can facilitate Terri's progress.

Over the next few months, Terri continues in the day program and openly expresses her satisfaction with it; however, she denies that she has any special interest in any particular staff members or patients. In family meetings, she expresses concern about activities after she leaves the day program. She enrolls in an evening and weekend socialization program at another agency. In recounting the activities they offer, she reports that she does not think she is ready yet to take their class on dating etiquette. She also enrolls in a volleyball clinic and aerobic dancing classes at a nearby recreation center. She smilingly reports her enjoyment of these activities. The quality of the family meetings has greatly changed as Terri often brings an agenda of matters that she wants to discuss.

Thirty-Four Months. After discussing her interest in a job in the data entry field for several months, she obtains a temporary job for six weeks in this field through her own efforts and leaves the day treatment program. She successfully completes their weeklong training program in three days and reports finding this work satisfying. She continues to attend the socialization program and other recreation activities. Her parents report that acquaintances from these activities have begun to telephone Terri. She purchases a pedigreed puppy and becomes quite involved in its care.

Year Four

While continuing to work at seasonal employment in data entry (eight weeks on, five weeks off), Terri discontinues her other recreational activities. She abruptly loses interest in her puppy and gives this expensive animal to a local animal shelter. She offers no explanation for this impulsive action.

After about six months of increased withdrawal, Terri's name comes to the top of a residential program waiting list. This application had been made two years ago and had largely been forgotten. Although she is getting along well with her parents, she is enthusiastic about having the opportunity to move into her own apartment. She continues to work seasonally in data entry but has few other activities.

After several months of interviews and trial visits, Terri moves into a supervised apartment program. She is very pleased about this move but seems more excited about the concept of "independence" than the reality. She continues to work in data entry.

Year Five

About four months after her move, Terri announces her intention to quit her job in several days. Her residential program counselor joins our family meeting where this issue is discussed. We calmly point out that she will still have to have a day program to continue to reside in her apartment. She says she does not want to do anything and suggests she may just move to a homeless shelter to avoid returning to her parents.

In a phone conversation with her residential counselor, a summer intern, I learn that she had just completed an ambitious service plan with Terri. She accepts my suggestion that she scale this back. In another phone conversation with her mother, we decide that her mother will invite her to a movie and avoid discussion of her job. Three days later, Terri returns to work. We also learn that because she has been "gainfully employed" for nine months, her SSDI benefits are being cut off.

Sixty-Four Months. Terri calls me to request special assistance to help her obtain entry to a local day program during her layoff period at her seasonal job. As she rarely contacts me outside our monthly family meetings, this is an unusual occurrence. I arrange an individual meeting to complete a lengthy application form.

Soon after, a new residential counselor calls me to report that Terri is isolating herself in the apartment. In our family meeting, Terri indicates that she has refused a special assignment at her job and is beginning a day program within several days. She says she would prefer to do nothing every day, but contacted this day program because daily activity is part of the treatment contract of her residential program. Several weeks after her admission, I attend a treatment planning meeting at the day program. Within a week, Terri quits the day program, saying she is bored. A week later, she returns to her data entry job.

Sixty-Eight Months. Terri continues to do well at her job and her residential placement. She is socializing more with other program members and has confided in her residential counselor that she would eventually like a boyfriend. She invites a roommate to her parents' home during the Christmas holidays.

Seventy Months. Terri is told that her residential counselor is transferring to another unit in her agency. Within a week, Terri decides to leave the program and return home. She also quits her job and again announces she is not interested in employment.

Before convening an emergency family meeting, I confer with Terri's residential counselor and psychiatrist. Given her past history, we try to respond calmly to this latest crisis. In the family meeting, I state that I think she was upset about the fifth change of residential counselor in the past year. She denies this and says she has no interest in people or work. Her family is also upset because her grandfather's health is deteriorating, and he may have to come live with them. Within two weeks, she says she is bored and joins a health spa. She faithfully works out four or five times a week.

Informing Terri of my plan—which she says she does not care about—I write a letter to the director of the residential program, protesting the repeated change in workers. The assistant director of the agency responds, apologizes for all the changes, and agrees to convene a family meeting to address these concerns. He also proposes a way that Terri can continue her relationship with her residential counselor.

Year Six

A week later, the residential program convenes a family meeting, and Terri agrees to continue working with her residential counselor although she still wants to live with her parents. She says she does not want to live with other mentally ill persons but will consider a supported living arrangement. In our family meeting, she says she would like another job, and we discuss several possibilities. Within four days, she obtains a part-time job selling women's clothes in a department store. She reports that she greatly enjoys this job.

Seventy-Six Months. We are meeting every four to six weeks because of Terri's shifting work schedule. Terri reports that she began working full time in the department store after a month and was permanently assigned to the lingerie department. While she would previously focus in a perfectionistic manner on her vocational shortcomings, she now openly takes pride in her accomplishments and expresses pleasure with her job.

Living at home with her parents in a mutually rewarding relationship, she envisions herself obtaining her own apartment at some point in the future. She meets monthly with her psychiatrist and continues on a low dose of a conventional neuroleptic medication. She also meets weekly with the residential counselor to discuss her daily activities and to participate in some recreational activities. More than at any time since I have known her, she exhibits a radiant smile, a lively wit, and an interest in the world around her.

Discussion

Terri's treatment and recovery process illustrates the role of the case manager in collaborating with a supportive family. While case management is most often associated with mentally ill clients with nonexistent, severely damaged, or malevolent social networks, the majority of these individuals do have families who are willing to provide substantial levels of support yet need consultation and support themselves (Bernheim and Lehman, 1985; Kanter, 1985a). In many situations, like the B. family, relatives are actually the primary "case managers" and prefer to share this responsibility with a professional case manager rather than discontinue their caregiving abruptly.

However, as a professional, I was able to perform certain case management activities that would have been difficult for Mr. and Mrs. B. to perform, most notably in forming linkages to psychiatrists, day and residential programs, and hospitals. As a professional, I was able to establish more direct and candid communication with these caregivers than most families would find possible, and importantly, I was able to offer many of them consultation that enabled all parties to sustain a coherent long-term treatment approach.

Similarly, as Terri recovered, she increasingly became her own case manager, exploring day program options, finding her own jobs, and joining a health club with little external assistance. Titrating the levels of support, I offered less and less assistance as the recovery process evolved, only becoming more active when crises ensued (Kanter, 1985b, 1987, 1989).

From the beginning, I saw my primary role as a consultant to Mr. and Mrs. B. and rarely attempted to intervene on an individual basis with Terri. During these six years, I only had three contacts with Terri without her parents present: one session she requested to get my help with applying to a day treatment program; one visit to see her apartment in the residential program; and one treatment planning conference at a day program. Yet, she would tell staff from other programs that I was her therapist, implying that I have a psychic significance for her that she has never expressed to me directly.

My relationship with Terri and her family was almost always casual and nonintensive, with neither strong transference nor countertransference. Of course, Terri devalued any contact with me for several years, but this response was characteristic of her schizoid devaluation of any human connection. While she was angry at me during several early crises, this anger was quickly repressed and was never discussed. I sometimes commented that Terri seemed unhappy with a particular action or suggestion of mine, but she repeatedly denied that she had any anger toward me, and I generally avoided challenging this defense (Meyer, 1988).

My main interpretative interactions with Terri were in gently, but repeatedly, commenting that her schizoid defenses—her lack of interest in people or activity—were an effective way of protecting herself against further disappointments. She often would dismiss these comments, and again, I would not confront her defenses. However, I would return again and again to this theme. After her recovery was well underway, I went somewhat further on this theme when, during a relapse, she again insisted that she had no interest in social relationships. I told Terri directly that she was "once a loving and lovable little girl" who sought contact with others. When she denied this, I turned to Mrs. B. who vividly reminisced about Terri's childhood desires for social relatedness. Similarly, my recent intervention with her residential program around the repeated changes of staff was an attempt to acknowledge the hurt these transitions had done to the shy child who was beginning to reemerge.

The development of my rapport with Mr. and Mrs. B. also deserves some attention. This case was treated in my private practice, and my work was paid for by the family. In contrast to the initial contact of an assigned case in a clinic setting, a respected professional had referred them to me, and they read my booklet for relatives soon after we met (Kanter, 1984a). Thus, we were able to begin working together with a level of confidence that might have taken months to develop in a clinic setting. However, the content and intensity of my interventions were not different from my usual practice in a busy agency—about twelve to thirty hours a year.

From the beginning, our meetings have always begun with ten to thirty minutes of quasi-social conversation, discussing movies, books, television shows, current events, family gatherings, and similar interests. Sometimes, these topics involved African-American personalities or interests.

On a surface level, these conversations could be viewed as technique for joining with the family. However, from the beginning, they reflected a more ambitious therapeutic effort to address Terri's schizoid defense, a condition more commonly referred to as negative symptoms or a deficit syndrome. Drawing on my earlier work in day treatment (Kanter, 1984b), these casual conversations we̊re an attempt to operationalize Winnicott's (1971) concepts about the therapeutic impact of play. From the first meetings in my office, I was trying to facilitate the development of a mutually pleasurable relationship between Terri and her parents. To accomplish this, I did not want to encourage the anguished dialogues characteristic of traditional family therapy or the didactic atmosphere implicit in more contemporary psychoeducational approaches. Thus, I invited the family out for a slice of pizza and later encouraged Mr. and Mrs. B. to fulfill Terri's request to visit an amusement park. The success of these outings soon inspired other activities that were initiated outside of our family meetings.

Although this sort of activity or dialogue can occur in individual psychotherapy (Frederickson, 1991), it can be difficult for the therapist to sustain a playful attitude without reinforcement from the client. However, in a family, group, or milieu setting, case managers can find other partners who are capable of engaging in playful activity or interaction. Clients can observe this interaction for months and eventually begin to participate without the caregivers succumbing to boredom or despair. When clients do begin to participate, they begin to enjoy themselves again in the company of others, a profound healing experience. Of course, in this situation, the bulk of this work occurs at home between our meetings.

Finally, Terri's recovery from schizophrenia, though not yet complete raises questions about our treatment goals and expectations with similar clients. Her relatively successful premorbid history would suggest a higher likelihood of a good outcome (Fenton and McGlashan, 1987), but her persistent deficit syndrome would suggest the likelihood of a poorer outcome. However, in spite of the severity of her illness, early intervention, involving at different points in time medication, case management, family consultation, hospitalization, day treatment, and residential support, was able to mobilize family resources and eventually Terri's own considerable abilities. In doing so, Terri has made major strides toward developing a real life in the community, not merely a marginal existence with troubling residual symptoms and make-work activities.

References

Bernheim, K. F., and Lehman, A. F. *Working with Families of the Mentally Ill.* New York: Norton, 1985.

Fenton, W. S., and McGlashan, T. H. "Prognostic Scale for Chronic Schizophrenia." *Schizophrenia Bulletin,* 1987, *13,* 277–286.

Frederickson, J. "From Delusion to Play." *Clinical Social Work Journal,* 1991, *19* (4), 349–362.

Kanter, J. S. *Coping Strategies for Relatives of the Mentally Ill.* Arlington, Va.: National Alliance for the Mentally Ill, 1984a.

Kanter, J. S. "Resocialization in Schizophrenia: Renegotiating the Latency Era." *International Review of Psycho-Analysis,* 1984b, *11,* 43–59.

Kanter, J. S. "Consulting with Families of the Chronic Mentally Ill." In J. S. Kanter (ed.), *Clinical Issues in Treating the Chronic Mentally Ill.* New Directions for Mental Health Services, no. 27. San Francisco: Jossey-Bass, 1985a.

Kanter, J. S. "The Process of Change in the Chronic Mentally Ill: A Naturalistic Perspective." *Psychosocial Rehabilitation Journal,* 1985b, *9* (1), 55–69.

Kanter, J. S. "Titrating Support in Case Management." *Tie-Lines,* 1987, *4* (4), 5–6.

Kanter, J. S. "Clinical Case Management: Definition, Principles, Components." *Hospital and Community Psychiatry,* 1989, *40,* 361–368.

Meyer, W. S. "On the Mishandling of 'Anger' in Psychotherapy." *Clinical Social Work Journal,* 1988, *16* (4), 406–417.

Winnicott, D. W. *Playing and Reality.* London: Tavistock, 1971.

JOEL KANTER, M.S.W., L.C.S.W., is a senior case manager on the comprehensive support services unit of the Mount Vernon Center for Community Mental Health, Fairfax County, Virginia.

Commentary

Kayla F. Bernheim, Ph.D.
Private Practitioner
Avon, New York

This case begins in a way that is familiar to those of us who have ever worked in a community mental health center: parents call us, frantic about their young adult child whose behavior has become increasingly reclusive, bizarre, and frightening. They receive with disbelief and dismay our "sorry, there's nothing we can do because your daughter (or son) doesn't want help and isn't a danger to self or others." How can it be that someone so obviously ill can not be helped? Terri B. and her family did get help—meaningful help—and the story of how that happened contains several useful lessons for clinicians working with persons with chronic mental illness.

Trust has to be earned through stability, reliability, and availability. Clinicians often label patients' or families' unwillingness to do what we suggest as "resistance" or "sabotage" or lack of motivation. Often, however, we have failed to demonstrate sufficient interest, competence, or caring to justify their trusting us.

In the public mental health system, it is quite rare for a patient or family to have the luxury of working with the same clinician for over five years. This case illustrates how valuable such a long-term relationship can be to a person with a long-term illness.

Kanter's steadfastness, manifested in his availability at times of crisis, his willingness to go to the home, and his consistent meetings with the family during good times and bad, allowed him to function effectively as family consultant and ombudsman. For example, his suggestion that the B's refuse to take Terri home from the hospital unless she agreed to certain conditions would be extremely difficult for most families to carry out. However, after five months of relationship-building, along with Kanter's presence during the meetings, they were able to implement this successfully. His willingness to collaborate with and coordinate a myriad of other caregivers represents clinical case management at its best, further enhancing his relationship with both patient and family.

If you can't do what you want, do what you can. Initially, Kanter tried to establish a relationship with Terri so that he could get her into treatment. No doubt he would have liked to see her hospitalized, or at least medicated. Neither was possible, but unlike most clinicians, he did not stop there. Instead, he continued to stay in contact with the B's, earning their trust and enabling him to mobilize them effectively when a crisis occurred.

When Terri proved unwilling to discuss illness-related issues in family meetings, Kanter was willing to spend six months mostly "chatting casually" with her parents. Most of us (and most insurance companies) would hardly regard this as "therapy," but I suspect it was invaluable in helping to contain the family's anxiety and in helping the parents develop realistic expectations. It may also have functioned, as Kanter suggests, to address Terri's deficit syndrome through modeling. It certainly set the kind of nonthreatening, "low EE" (Vaughn and others, 1984) tone that facilitates reconstitution from acute psychosis. With the family's support, facilitated by Kanter, Terri was able to stay out of the hospital for a full year until, under the self-imposed pressure of thinking about going to work, she relapsed. It is interesting to speculate whether this outcome would have been different had the family had to cope with their child's symptomatology, as so many still do, with little professional guidance and support. The research literature (Anderson, Reiss, and Hogarty, 1986; Falloon and others, 1981) suggests it would have.

If flexible roles and boundaries make you nervous, think about working with a different population. Consider the long list of Kanter's unorthodoxies: his initial meeting is two hours in length, he makes three home visits, he takes the family out during a "therapy" session and buys the patient pizza, he attends meetings at other agencies and invites other involved professionals to his family meetings, he gives very specific, directive advice, he helps the patient fill out a form and accompanies her to an interview, he writes an indignant letter to a residential program director, he talks to the parents about the patient behind her back. He appears to neither know, nor care, whose therapist he is—or indeed, whether he is a family therapist, case manager, or family consultant. There are certainly pitfalls possible in this sort of seat-of-the-pants, pragmatic approach, and I am tempted to warn (as they do in the commercials), "Don't try this at home!"

How did Terri feel about Kanter's strong alliance with her parents and how did it affect her ability to relate to the treatment system? How did Terri's psychiatrist feel about Kanter's intervening with the residential counselor to scale back the service plan? How did he decide that he, rather than Terri or her parents, should complain about the frequent change of residential counselors? How would Kanter respond to a genuine conflict of interest between Terri and her parents? These are the kinds of questions that Kanter was probably considering as he went along. Most case managers lack Kanter's years of experience, so strong supervision and collegial support should be provided to help clinicians think through the loyalty, ethical, and practical issues that are bound to arise.

Timing is everything. Even, uninterrupted progress is rare in the life of the young adult with schizophrenia. Terri B. had numerous setbacks during the five years covered by this case report. These tended to occur whenever she experienced the expectation, external or internal, of a higher level of functioning. Kanter showed unusual patience and persistence, keeping his focus on the long haul rather than on day-to-day perturbations in Terri's clinical condition or level of motivation. He modeled for the family (and treatment team) an emotionally measured response, not overreacting to the patient's inevitable resistances and fears, nor succumbing to hopelessness about her chances for substantial recovery. Choosing when to intervene with the treatment system is particularly delicate— inappropriately timed interventions can engender resistance while holding back risks allowing an unnecessary exacerbation of symptoms to occur. Kanter's case report does not give us a direct window into how he chose when to intervene, but the two examples of intervention he provides are instructive. In one, he acted to reduce the functional expectations for Terri. In another, he acted to preserve what had become a strong therapeutic alliance Terri had developed with a residential counselor. Indeed, modulating the levels of stress and expectation and fostering positive interpersonal connections are important goals in working with this population.

Take a holistic approach. "Treat the whole person." "Use a biopsychosocial model." These maxims are difficult to put into practice in an often fragmented mental health system. Level of psychiatric symptoms, work readiness, social supports, and personal motivations may be very weakly correlated, but each is relevant to the patient's capacity for rehabilitation. Kanter always kept sight of the "whole elephant," coordinating psychiatric, residential, vocational, and counseling services as well as trying to understand Terri's needs within her cultural, familial, and stage-of-life frames.

His knowledge of and interaction with the family was, I believe, critical to his success. The family is the repository of a great deal of useful information, not only about the development of the illness and current level of functioning, but about the patient as a person. Family members also constitute the inner hub of the patient's support network. While it is true that some chronically mentally ill individuals are abandoned by or lose contact with their families, many more maintain ties with parents and siblings. Indeed, many relatives function as integral parts of the caregiving network. As such, family members should be regarded and treated as valuable members of the treatment team (Bernheim and Lehman, 1985).

This case illustrates how family-based clinical case management, when carried out by a seasoned, flexible, attentive, and assertive clinician over an extended period of time, can contribute to the reintegration into life of a severely impaired person. In addition to the lessons it teaches, the case raises the fundamental question: What is success? After five years, Terri is again living at home. Has she failed at the fundamental task of living independently? I prefer to see her as having succeeded, at least for now, at living interdependently and in a mutually satisfying way with loved ones. She has a life that provides her with some rewards and is not an undue burden on others. To me, this is success aplenty.

Commentary References

Anderson, C. M., Reiss, D. J., and Hogarty, G. E. *Schizophrenia and the Family.* New York: Guilford Press, 1986.

Bernheim, K. F., and Lehman, A. F. *Working with Families of the Mentally Ill.* New York: Norton, 1985.

Falloon, I.R.H., Boyd, J. L., McGill, C. W., Strang, J. S., and Moss, H. B. "Family Management Training in the Community Care of Schizophrenia." In M. J. Goldstein (ed.), *New Developments in Interventions with Families of Schizophrenics.* New Directions for Mental Health Services, no. 12. San Francisco: Jossey-Bass, 1981.

Vaughn, C. E., Snyder, K. S., Jones, S., Freeman, W., and Falloon, I.R.H. "Family Factors in Schizophrenic Relapse." *Archives of General Psychiatry,* 1984, *41,* 1169–1177.

Sometimes assertive outreach is not enough; this case report
describes a ten-year effort to engage an often homeless,
alcoholic schizophrenic man.

Steven: Testing the Limits of Assertive Community Treatment

David Mays
Commentary by Charles R. Goldman

When Steven walked out of the maximum security section of the Mendota Mental Health Institute, he had been clean and sober for three straight months. He was taking an antipsychotic again, his diet was good, and he had gotten used to sleeping in a bed. He was also furious at me (his psychiatrist), at his inpatient team, at his outpatient team, and at everyone else who had been involved in his treatment. The outpatient team was exasperated with the inpatient team. The inpatient team was disgusted with the outpatient team. Everybody was disappointed with me. And Steven looked better than I had ever seen him.

Steven had been living as an inpatient at Mendota since a cold streak in January put his life in jeopardy and we, his caregivers, had contrived to get him arrested and sent to the state hospital to have his competency evaluated. The process had been a difficult and trying one, requiring an enormous amount of work by the mental health and legal systems combined. Steven did not appreciate the trouble and expense we had all gone to.

Steven experienced his first psychotic break in 1968 at the age of twenty-two. He voluntarily sought admission to a hospital because he was no longer able to function in college. His concentration had failed him, he was anxious, and he said he wanted "a rest." He thought some "psychoanalysis" might help him work out his relationship with his mother and, in passing, deal with a "little trouble" he was having with alcohol. Steven's mother was schizophrenic. She was living in a nursing home, and Steven had very little contact with her. He had been raised by foster parents. His father was unemployed and reportedly in a VA hospital somewhere with a heart condition.

NEW DIRECTIONS FOR MENTAL HEALTH SERVICES, no. 65, Spring 1995 © Jossey-Bass Publishers

At the time of his first hospitalization, Steven had been a student at the university in accounting, getting along on very little money. Not much is recorded about his friendships or social life in those early records. What we know is that he was diagnosed as having undifferentiated schizophrenia, he rubbed his forehead a lot, and he became quite a management problem on the unit. He was agitated and dissatisfied with the treatment offered; he tried to elope and pushed for early discharge. He got the discharge in six weeks, along with large doses of Stelazine and Thorazine.

The next we hear of Steven, it is 1969, and he is back in Mendota, after having been committed in Idaho for bizarre, paranoid behavior—he was twenty-three, and he thought people were trying to poison him. In Idaho, he had received nine electroconvulsive treatments, as well as enormous doses of drugs. Idaho sent him back to Wisconsin as soon as it could. This time he was discharged from Mendota fairly quickly and told to go to the local mental health center for follow-up.

He stayed away, of course. Five months later he was picked up by the police for vagrancy and for being mentally ill. Throughout the 1970s, Steven was regularly admitted to the state hospital. The records show him becoming increasingly grandiose, loose in his associations, confused, paranoid, psychotic, and in the end completely disorganized. In 1975, Steven was referred to the Program for Assertive Community Treatment (PACT) in Madison, a well-known outpatient treatment program that works with clients who have severe ongoing psychiatric disabilities.

The referral "didn't work out," says the record. In 1981, after a long procession of detoxification admissions for a growing alcohol problem, it was recommended that Steven be considered for involuntary protective services through the Dane County Mental Health Center. In other words, he would have a guardian appointed to make decisions about his housing, his finances, and his medication. Steven resisted these efforts. On the way to the proceedings, he jumped out of the car and was moderately injured. Nevertheless, in September 1981, Steven was committed under a guardianship to the Mobile Community Treatment Unit at the Mental Health Center of Dane County. The guardianship was to be reviewed yearly but to continue indefinitely.

Mobile Community Treatment (MCT) was started the same year that Steven entered the program. Its role was to function as one of the four prongs of mental health care provided to Dane County by the community mental health clinic. The three other services included emergency services, general clinical services, and a rehabilitation service. The specific goal of MCT was to provide intensive outpatient team-oriented services to clients with psychotic illnesses who experienced frequent, repetitive hospitalization. It was based on the model of the PACT program. There were 120 clients initially admitted to the program.

MCT ultimately evolved into two teams, each consisting of five case managers (usually social workers and a nurse), a team leader/case manager, a part-time psychiatrist, a psychiatric resident in training, and as many students as could be rounded up from the university in any given semester. The number of clients on each team was kept to sixty.

Over the years, the philosophy of MCT has remained constant in most respects. The primary focus has always been service to the client and the approach has always been to provide that service in the community. It has been known for some time that whatever skills needed to be taught to clients—shopping, cleaning, socializing, and so forth—needed to be taught in the context and environment where they would be used. And we believed that true independence and dignity for our clients could only be achieved in an outpatient setting. By contrast, hospitalization was viewed as a necessary evil, to be used only as a last resort. Hospitalization was expensive, regressive, and a failure of the case management system.

Unlike a typical medical clinic staff, the Mental Health Center staff is very egalitarian. A polite, consensus-driven style of management prevails, as it often does in the Midwest, with the senior members of the team usually having the most influence. The psychiatrist of the team is often given the last word when he or she is there. Of course, for economic reasons, the psychiatrist is rarely there. Consequently the medical model and the rehabilitation model peaceably coexist, and a non-M.D. democracy prevails in day-to-day treatment.

I first met Steven in 1984, when I was a psychiatric resident in training doing a rotation at MCT. At that point, he had been a client in the program for three years. He was on regular Prolixin shots, complained constantly about how he was controlled by "the system," and disliked doctors intensely. The progression of his illness had been halted, however, and he had not been hospitalized since his admission to the program. There was little evidence that he was being rehabilitated, however. His hygiene was unimaginably poor, he was not employed, and he had few if any personal relationships. And he was not interested in working with anyone on any issue for any period of time.

Steven would meet with me only if I took him out for coffee at the restaurant of his choice. MCT encouraged this kind of breakdown of traditional doctor-patient boundaries. The idea was that the more time in the community the resident doctors spent with the clients, the more sensitive the doctors would become to the range of difficulties the clients faced. Witnessing firsthand an individual's strengths, weaknesses, and coping and noncoping skills brought to life the concept that the relationship was as important as the medication in making interventions related to improving quality of life. We needed to meet our clients where they lived—literally.

These meetings usually occurred about every two months. Since I was paying, Steven would make a point of choosing the most expensive place available. Steven had an "in your face" attitude that precluded any embarrassment on his part as we walked into the coffee shops. He would inevitably ask to be seated next to the best-dressed people there. He smelled terrible, dressed worse, and would proceed to carry on loudly about police and political repression. I tried to act natural. The time passed slowly.

Our best meetings were when we talked about books that he was reading.

He had no one else to talk to about the things that were important to him—*The Greening of America* or *The Last Temptation of Christ*. He came to accept me because he learned I had been an English teacher before I became a psychiatrist. So we developed a relationship—not exactly friendly but close to friendly.

I left MCT at the end of my rotation in 1984, but returned in 1990 as the medical director of Mobile Community Treatment, after completing my residency and spending three years in private practice. I recognized many of my old clients but not Steven. I was struck by how much he had changed for the worse. His body and mouth odor made it impossible to be in an enclosed room with him—my eyes would water and I would literally gag from the smell. He was obviously drinking more or at least drinking more obviously. He tried to talk about books he was reading but could not hold a thought together long enough to express it. He was still on high doses of Prolixin and was beginning to develop tardive dyskinesia. The MCT team felt frustrated with him as well as hopeless about him. Among other irritations, the team would spend weeks locating an apartment for Steven, who would then be evicted in a matter of days because of his behavior. (He would start his mattress on fire by careless smoking, for instance.) His alcoholism was out of control. MCT controlled his money, but he managed to panhandle enough cash to be drunk all the time anyway. If he was given grocery money, he spent it on beer. If he was given groceries, he sold them and bought beer. None of us could think of anything to do. For his part, Steven denied there were any problems except for our nagging control over his life.

Over the next year, Steven and I met occasionally. I hoped, somewhat egocentrically, that he would begin to improve in order to please me, his old friend. However, the only rapport we ever established was when he twice let me read some of his confused religious writings. In fact, the only way he would see me at all was if MCT paid him $5 a session. (Imagine my chagrin when it was announced at the team meeting one day that we were putting a block on his phone because he had spent $800 calling a Joyce Brothers 900 number!)

He developed a confrontational relationship with me as he had with the rest of the team. He would frequently yell at each team member in turn, especially if we were handing out his money. He accused us of stealing from him, espoused revolutionary slogans, and proclaimed himself a political prisoner.

Over the next two years, a team consensus evolved that viewed Steven's primary problem as alcoholism, not schizophrenia. This change in viewpoint was gradual and somewhat subtle. Whenever we saw Steven, he was drunk. By the same token, we rarely observed any psychotic symptoms that could be distinguished from his intoxicated behavior. Of course, any psychotic symptoms would have been fairly well muted by the regular high doses of Prolixin he received. Nonetheless, we ceased thinking of him as schizophrenic. In retrospect, we may have been coping with our helplessness by labeling Steven as an alcoholic rather than a schizophrenic. Lacking the power to cure him, we could feel less guilty about our failed interventions if we diagnosed him as an alcoholic who was responsible in a direct way for his behavior.

For whatever reason, we were no longer convinced the Prolixin was helping him. Additionally, I was worried about the combination of alcohol with his medication, as well as his potential for worsening tardive dyskinesia, especially with a medicine that was not clearly necessary. With the team's agreement, I started lowering his medication. By November 1992, his Prolixin was stopped completely, and he was no longer on any prescription drugs. Steven continued to drink and continued to repeat over and over, as he had for the last two years, "Give me some money"; "Have you got anything for me?" "What can you do for me?"—basically, his panhandling phrases. There was virtually no change in his presentation when he was off the Prolixin.

Because of his poor hygiene, Steven developed a severe dermatitis on his face, arms, and feet that required antibiotics. We forced him to soak his feet when he came in for his daily cash, and threw away his old socks, giving him new ones daily. We tried to dress the lesions on his face and hands when he would let us. Watching Steven literally begin to rot in front of us was a terrible experience. We spent hours trying to come up with something that would get Steven to change. Half the team would argue that we should stop rescuing (enabling) him so that he would hit bottom. Then, they argued, he would be forced into more responsible behavior. The other half of the team would reply that if this wasn't the bottom, they didn't know what was, and argued that we should take complete charge over Steven's life and get him committed to a locked facility. We went over and over the same questions: Did he need antipsychotics? (No.) Should we help him find yet another place to live, after we told him the last time was the last time? (Probably.) Are we absolutely certain we can't get an alcohol commitment? (I'll call the corporation counsel again, but I'm sure.)

As Steven became less desirable to be around, he was inevitably around more. At times, he seemed to be asking for help. We responded, but he was never able to follow through, no matter what we did, and we simply were not able to be with him twenty-four hours a day. The manager of our city's alcohol detoxification program called to scold us. He pointed out that Steven had set a record with sixty-one admissions to detox (brought in by the police), and he wondered why we were not doing anything about it. We invited the detox staff in for a conference. Did they have any ideas? (No.) The police told us it was not unusual for them to find Steven bloodied and unconscious. Once, the police told us, they had chased off a man who was trying to strangle him. Steven had no memory of any of this and loudly insisted he was once again being persecuted by the state. Unbelievably, his laboratory work was normal. There was not enough evidence for a civil commitment. He was not in imminent danger.

January 1994 was especially cold in Wisconsin. The temperature had been fluctuating between zero and twenty-seven below. Since Steven was refusing to stay at the room we had gotten for him at a local motel, we suspected he was living in the street and each morning dreaded hearing the news that he had frozen to death during the night.

When the temperature hit twenty-three below zero for two days in a row, and was falling with wind chills to fifty below, we could stand it no more. When Steven showed up at MCT to pick up his money, loud and obnoxious, instead of ignoring him, we provoked him. With several members of the team standing in close enough proximity, he ended up shoving a caseworker. We called the police. Steven fled. Five members of the team swore out a complaint against him. The police, quite cooperative, found Steven on the street shortly after. He resisted arrest and was taken to jail.

In consultation with the jail mental health assessment team, we suggested that rather than be released to our custody, as would usually be the case, Steven should be sent to the hospital to be evaluated for competency to stand trial. He was sent to the forensic assessment unit at the Mendota Mental Health Institute for his first hospitalization in thirteen years. We felt guilty because we had never contrived to have someone arrested before. We felt relieved because he was safe.

In addition to working part time as the medical director of MCT, I am also the forensic medical director at the Mendota Mental Health Institute. I am the unit psychiatrist on the Management Unit (MU), which is the unit in maximum security that handles the fourteen most violent and difficult patients in the state. The unit is very staff intensive, low stimulation, and structured. Patients are permitted few possessions and privileges. Treatment plans are written and implemented by teams with the psychiatrist and unit chief (a psychologist) providing leadership to the nurse manager and nursing staff, occupational therapists, and social workers. Unlike the Mental Health Center, roles are very hierarchical.

Most of the patients admitted to this unit start out wearing leather wrist restraints called Passive Aggression Devices (PADS). These restraints keep peers and staff safe while we evaluate new admissions, and help us de-escalate violent patients while still allowing them to socialize and interact out of their rooms. This minimizes the use of seclusion, which can make many psychotic illnesses worse. Patients earn their way out of PADS by following a very basic set of rules successfully for seven consecutive days. They are locked in their rooms at night and eat in their rooms as well.

Like all new admissions, Steven was first hospitalized on the maximum security unit but was specifically referred to MU. This occurred for two reasons: Steven was fighting fairly aggressively when he was brought into Mendota, and I wanted him on the unit where I worked.

Steven's admission highlighted the contrast of my two jobs. Several days each week, I work with a progressive, consumer-oriented outpatient team designed to help people live with as much autonomy as possible. For the remainder, I work in the most restrictive, control-oriented inpatient unit in the state. As a rule, I feel little conflict between these two roles. I simply leave one well-circumscribed job and go to another. When Steven came to the unit, however, my two different worlds collided.

It was painful to see Steven locked on a unit, as he loved nothing more than to be pleasantly adrift in the city. Now that he was safe, I began to feel guilty and responsible for his misery. I was also distressed as the MU inpatient team met the MCT outpatient team. They eyed each other with curiosity and skepticism and then looked at me. It was like having your in-laws meet for the first time—cordial, but distant. With the MCT team looking at our security-oriented, very "unnormalized" space, I was suddenly embarrassed. I wanted to let Steven go. Getting him admitted at all had been a big mistake. At the same time, the MU staff asked me questions about what kind of outpatient team would let a patient regularly drink himself stuporous, live on the street, and live in such filth. I tried to explain the legal dilemmas and was embarrassed all over again.

Steven, for his part, did not like MU at all, and he let us know in the most obnoxious ways he could. He would smear feces in his room, throw his food, and until the very eve of his discharge, he would stand by his door whenever it was locked and yell, "Guard! Let me out of here!" He aggravated even the most hardened MU staff members. It was extremely annoying.

Of course, Steven was pretty annoyed himself. He could not smoke, he could not drink, and he could not come and go as he pleased. He could not panhandle spare change from the other patients on the unit, either, although he tried. We regularly had to escort him to his room for his own safety, as fellow patients reached the end of their tolerance. These were not peers to be around when they reached the end of their tolerance.

The manifest goal of this admission was to assess Steven's competency to stand trial, but we were really interested in performing a more comprehensive assessment of Steven, off alcohol, while he was living in a stable environment. Steven's conversation over the past year had been limited to those few stock panhandling phrases: "What have you got for me?" "Are you going to help me out?" and "Can't help you." He repeated these phrases no matter what the context. We wondered how much brain damage might have occurred through alcohol, beatings, accidents, or lifestyle. Another goal was to determine whether or not Steven would benefit from psychiatric medication. I was bothered by the fact that while I had not seen a clear difference in Steven off Prolixin, I knew by his history that he clearly had suffered from a psychotic illness at some point. Had the Prolixin been exerting a subtle benefit that we had missed in the constant drama of his ongoing crises? Would a different antipsychotic be more helpful? Finally, although we were keeping Steven alive during the winter, and I doubted he could survive many nights at twenty below zero, Steven himself seemed to not care whether he lived or died. Was this depression? Alcoholism? Organicity? A combination?

The first activity for patients on MU when they have come from the jail is to take a "kwell" shower to kill any lice. Of course, Steven refused to take a shower voluntarily for several days. We then helped him with the shower and with showers every several days after that. He needed less encouragement with each succeeding shower. It was hard to tell if that was because he began to enjoy being clean or because he gave up resisting. I had never seen Steven clean in all the years I had known him. I literally did not recognize him sitting in the dayroom the day after his first shower. He had long blond hair, a fluffy beard, and clean clothes. I actually asked the staff who the new admission was. They told me to go find out, and my mouth dropped when I recognized him. He grinned, then started in again asking for money, "Are you going to help me out?"

This should not be taken as an early turning point. Steven had always been a management nightmare as an inpatient. His passive/aggressive side blossomed in this restrictive environment. When he did not get something he wanted, he would urinate all over the floor. He would snap his fingers as the nurse tried to get his blood pressure. He was so abusive in phone calls to his lawyer that the lawyer, a patient man, finally quit in disgust. He would go into other patients' rooms to use their toilets. He refused to have any contact with me or the staff except to demand his liberty, beg for spare change, ask to be left alone, or complain about being left alone. Finally, he complained that everyone was always telling him to shut up. We tried to give him some feedback.

"Can't help you," said Steven.

In a hearing fourteen days after admission, the court found Steven incompetent either to participate in his own defense in court or to make decisions about his medication. After six weeks without clinical or behavioral change, both the inpatient and outpatient teams were pushing for a trial of medication, any medication. I decided on Risperidone because of its novel antipsychotic properties and its low side-effect profile. We kept trying to impress upon Steven the importance of working with us instead of fighting against us, but he was invested only in his battle with the system. He took the medication because he hoped it would get him out of the hospital and back on the street, not because he expected it to make him feel better. Besides, he knew that we would force it on him anyway.

For my part, I felt pressured by the MU staff to do something. What they wanted was for me to get Steven out of the hospital. They were tired of his disruptions. They did not view him as dangerous enough for their unit. His crime had not been that serious. Interestingly, the MCT outpatient team members had fallen into a routine of visiting once a week and leaving quietly. It finally dawned on me that they were now fully engaged in new crises with other clients and were perfectly content to have someone else taking care of Steven. I felt like I was pushing MCT to get a plan for Steven's discharge at the same time I was arguing with MU that he did actually belong on their unit.

After two months on the ward and two weeks on the medication, Steven made a joke. I do not remember what it was, but I remember laughing with him and the staff. Later that week, at an MCT meeting, one of the case managers mentioned that Steven had actually sat and talked to her for fifteen minutes during her weekly visit. It was clear that Steven was improving.

In April, we sent a report to the court that Steven was marginally competent and as competent as he was ever likely to become. His case manager from MCT appeared with him at court and presented an outpatient plan to the judge. He was released on parole and told to avoid alcohol.

When he was released from the court, Steven immediately went out to have a drink, and he was drunk by that afternoon. We had great difficulty in securing him a place to live. His terrible reputation in the housing community did not disappear during his hospitalization. We scheduled three interviews with the only structured living group that would accept him, but he disappeared before each interview, and we could not find him.

He simply would not live anywhere where there were rules. For several weeks, Steven, who was living in a motel, maintained much better hygiene. He was friendlier with most of our staff than he had been for years. He was not particularly friendly with me, whom he blamed for keeping him as a political prisoner in Mendota. But he was taking his medicine, and even at one point asked for an increase because of "stress." We were unable to help him describe what he meant by stress. We tried ever so gently to talk about how his drinking could be contributing to his increasing dysphoria. He became defensive and angry and stomped out of the building. We gave him the increase in the medication anyway.

In the hospital, Steven had become far less persistent with his panhandling talk as he approached his discharge and was actually able to carry on a conversation with staff. He maintained this positive change for six weeks or so after his discharge. Then he began to slide into his old linguistic or cognitive confusion. We know now that this was a result of Steven's drinking rather than his schizophrenia. And we know now that Steven is capable of doing better than he is doing now. What we do not know is how to get this change to occur.

Discussion

The team sees Steven as suffering from three illnesses: He is schizophrenic. He is alcoholic. He is malignantly passive/aggressive. The schizophrenia is seen from his history and verified through the response we saw to antipsychotic medication while he was in the hospital. It is a part of his illness that we had gradually lost sight of as his alcoholism made him increasingly dysfunctional and demanding. The alcoholism makes its contribution by destroying Steven's judgment and initiative, fostering denial, and maiming his central nervous system. It is likely to kill him. Meanwhile, the passive/aggressive behavior stems from anger and a deep-seated feeling of unfairness. His interactional pattern is one of "set up and shoot down." Steven rejects our help and makes sure we fail in all our attempts to make his life better. But he keeps coming back and asking for us to do something for him. In this way, he is constantly getting at us. He asks for help, we provide it. It is never enough.

Steven's hospitalization allowed us to intervene at some level with all three of Steven's illnesses. We provided monitored medication. We enforced abstinence. We utilized a structure where Steven's interactional style changed because the hospital's rigidity limited the ways he could set us up. And his sense of unfairness was limited because everyone on the unit was in the same boat.

We were not able to provide continuity for this intensive treatment when he was released from the hospital. We were able to monitor his medication, but we could not keep him away from alcohol, and he soon fell back into his old passive/aggressive behavior.

Steven is presently in jail. His judge revoked his probation because of his continuing public drunkenness. Our team continues to visit him regularly. He is extremely unhappy. Another inmate hit him last week when he became obnoxious and overly intrusive. He wants to go back to Mendota where "everyone is nicer to him." He has been alcohol free for several weeks and is beginning to speak more clearly and show more affect. Last week, he actually cried during our interview. I am leaning strongly toward starting an antidepressant in the next few days. He continues on his antipsychotic.

So we are caught in a dilemma. We are a community support program, and it goes against our most fundamental beliefs to advocate long-term hospitalization. We consistently work toward collaboration instead of control with our clients, in outpatient not institutional settings. We believe that any treatment plan with Steven is doomed to failure unless it is Steven's plan for himself, not our plan for Steven.

On the other hand, to give Steven autonomy is to abandon him. He would have died last winter if we had not intervened. His illnesses have seriously impaired his initiative, his insight, and his self-esteem. The very heart of assertive community treatment is to be there persistently, not just to support but to fill in the ego gaps as needed to help clients function with as much dignity as possible.

So, if we take control of Steven's body for long enough, can we eventually win his heart? We surely will continue to get nowhere as long as Steven continues his adversarial relationship with us and his affiliative relationship with alcohol. Should we let him go and try to help him find his own way into a collaboration with us as we treat his schizophrenia, offering community support as we have been? People change. And Steven has shown us some brief glimmers of insight.

The sad reality is that this is not an academic discussion for our team. Steven's life hangs in the balance as we make decisions based on the realities of resource allocation, legal constraints, and our own individual capacities to keep giving. As Steven says, "Are you going to help me out?"

I do not know. We will do the best we can.

DAVID MAYS, M.D., Ph.D., is medical director of forensics at Mendota State Hospital and medical director of community support programs at the Mental Health Center of Dane County in Madison, Wisconsin. He is also assistant clinical professor of psychiatry, University of Wisconsin School of Medicine.

Commentary

Charles R. Goldman, M.D.
Director, Public Psychiatry Program
Department of Neuropsychiatry and Behavioral Science
University of South Carolina School of Medicine

This case is an excellent example of the frustrating dilemma assertive community-based clinicians frequently face: if we intervene aggressively, we risk losing the trust and cooperation of our client; yet if we follow his lead, we must helplessly watch him deteriorate. When we have the desire, obligation, and ability to help someone who not only rejects our sincere efforts but also leaves us feeling unappreciated and defensive, we feel set up—as if the object of our concern perversely delights in our pain and is willing to destroy himself just to see us suffer. Whether this is due to passive aggression, addiction, or paranoia—or to a difference in culture or values—matters less than the practical question posed by Mays: "If we take control of Steven's body for long enough, can we eventually win his heart?" Or are there ways we can force a client to cooperate and can this process lead to true collaboration?

Before offering some reflections about alternative treatment strategies in this situation, it is important to note that Mays and his colleagues have enjoyed partial success in establishing a therapeutic relationship with Steven. Although often resistant, Steven visits the agency offices, takes his prescribed medications, and cooperates to some extent with their efforts at money management. These are not insignificant accomplishments with such an intractably disturbed client. Yet I can certainly identify with the sense of helplessness and despair that is evoked when working with particular clients who seem to continuously frustrate our best efforts over many years.

With such help-rejecting and disabled clients, the engagement process requires many months, if not years. During this time, one or more clinicians meets with the client, often on his own turf, establishes rapport, elicits a short-term desire or goal that the clinician will help the client attain (such as better housing or getting a tooth fixed) and generally concentrates on building a therapeutic relationship. For a client with both mental illness and substance dependency, the clinician looks for opportunities to make contact during episodes of sobriety (that is, in a detox unit, jail, or hospital) but cannot expect continued sobriety at this point. Over time and in the context of a therapeutic relationship, the clinician gradually moves into a "persuasion" mode (Osher and Kofoed, 1989). Eventually, through a process involving "empathic detachment" and "empathic confrontation" (Minkoff, 1993), the client may become willing to at least examine whether substance use is helping or hindering the pursuit of life goals.

By becoming Steven's guardian, controlling his money, and meeting with him in his natural environment, the treatment team members were quite assertive, and partially successful, in their efforts to engage him. Even though there is some evidence that careful monitoring of clients correlates with satisfaction of services (Huxley and Warner, 1992), such techniques inevitably involve paternalistic or coercive elements. From both a clinical and ethical perspective, it is important that such interventions—taking control of a client's body—are aimed at improving his chances of survival, reducing the need for restrictive institutional confinement, and helping him improve his quality of life (Diamond and Wikler, 1985).

Although the staff clearly had these beneficial objectives in mind, Steven apparently had few complaints about his life, other than being controlled by the system. He valued his liberty and autonomy and "loved nothing more than to be pleasantly adrift in the city." It appears that the staff's objective criteria for a quality existence—safe and comfortable surroundings, a clear mind, basic hygiene—clashed with Steven's expressed criteria. But were his expressed wishes what he really wanted, or only what he had learned to settle for, given his failure to achieve what most people want? It is likely that he feared loss of freedom more than other dangers and deprivations, thus creating a vicious cycle where the more he struggled to be free the fewer choices he had, resulting in feeling more trapped and more need to struggle. All things considered, I believe it was clearly justified for the treatment team to act aggressively, without Steven's active consent, to take control of his body (including his brain) so he could ultimately make informed choices about his life. In my view, Steven's treatment could have been even more aggressive in order to more rapidly stop the vicious cycle and accelerate the process of recovery.

One of the most effective means of obtaining cooperation from clients like Steven is the strategic use of leverage, where clinicians exploit the natural consequences of self-destructive behavior (Nikkel and Coiner, 1991). When a crisis occurs, clients are shown several options for coping, at least one of which includes cooperation with treatment, sometimes even voluntary hospitalization. As Kanter (1985) has commented, change is frequently precipitated by the "psychic shocks" of our clients' real-life experiences (such as Steven's recent incarceration) rather than by planned treatment interventions. In this case, however, there was a surprising lack of consequences for Steven. In over ten years on the streets, he apparently was neither jailed nor involuntarily hospitalized until the past year, nor did his physical health deteriorate to the point of requiring hospitalization.

However, Steven did find his way into detox an astounding sixty-one times. I am curious about whether these detox crises could have been used more productively to begin a dialogue on the consequences of his alcohol abuse. This would have required a continuing, aggressive effort to work with detox staff and police to gain their trust, cooperation, and understanding. Also, there may even have been others in Steven's world who saw him on a weekly basis and could have been enlisted in a social network intervention and persuaded to participate in a leverage plan (Sokolove and Trimble, 1986).

In addition to capitalizing on such consequences, another intervention that would have helped is involuntary hospitalization. Early in the course of his illness, to escape the stress of college and what he recognized as a growing problem with alcohol, Steven sought hospitalization for himself. Later, he began to refuse voluntary hospitalization. He was hospitalized involuntarily only very late in the course of his illnesses and under extreme circumstances—criminal charges and a highly restrictive forensic unit. Even so, when faced with jail, he begged to return to the hospital where people were "nicer to him." This comment supports research findings that suggest that clients often come to appreciate involuntary treatment after its initiation (Schwartz, Vingiano, and Perez, 1988).

In my state, South Carolina, and in other states I am familiar with, involuntary commitment to either a substance abuse treatment facility or psychiatric hospital is available if the client's physical safety is in serious jeopardy and chronic substance abuse or mental illness is present. The biggest clinical disadvantage to involuntary hospitalization is that it may create an adversarial relationship between the client and members of the community treatment team. This risk can be minimized if other parties in the mental health system (such as emergency services staff) do the actual commitment and the community treatment team visits the hospital to discuss the natural consequences of the client's behavior.

In our outpatient dual diagnosis program, we have found that early, strategic use of brief hospital stays reduces overall hospital utilization and contributes to the eventual engagement of clients in community treatment (Goldman, Hicks, Bennett, and Leggett, 1994). Admission to a substance abuse treatment program rather than a psychiatric unit can significantly increase dually disordered clients' willingness to address issues related to their substance use. Besides ongoing collaboration with the staff of the substance abuse program, it is important to use appropriate medications, including long-acting injectable antipsychotics, to ameliorate disruptive psychotic symptoms. Given the powerful ideology of deinstitutionalization in his city (Wasow, 1993), I am not sure whether these options were available for Steven.

Earlier and more extensive use of both leverage and hospitalization might have presented opportunities for staff to persuade Steven that his alcohol use and oppositional behavior were interfering with his freedom. I also wonder whether more formal use of psychotherapy or psychotherapeutic techniques would have helped, especially since he requested this on his first admission in 1968 and later spent $800 of his limited funds calling Joyce Brothers. I am sure the Madison staff attempted to counsel Steven, but I cannot help wondering how his interest in psychotherapy could have been utilized to engage him in a treatment process. Although it is rarely the primary treatment, psychotherapy of serious mental illness and alcohol dependency can be very helpful (Coursey, 1989; Drake, McHugo, and Noordsy, 1993; Miller and Rollnick, 1991; Kanter, 1988; Lewis and Rosenberg, 1990; Prochaska, DiClemente, and Norcross, 1992; Wasylenki, 1992; Weiden and Havens, 1994).

In summary, the treatment team's eventual use of leverage and involuntary hospitalization did in many ways take control of Steven's body and give team members the opportunity to engage him in a treatment and rehabilitation process. I have suggested that these methods, plus use of psychotherapeutic and psychoeducational techniques, could have been used earlier and more extensively than they were. If, over time, the clinicians also convey their deeply felt caring and respect for Steven, they would have a shot at winning his cooperation, if not his heart. This conclusion is not likely to be news to Mays, but I hope it reinforces what he and the other clinicians already know and, in many ways, have already done.

I would like to make one final observation about the role of the psychiatrist. This case was presented from the perspective of a psychiatrist who was part of, but also apart from, the client's community treatment team. Mays states, "The psychiatrist is rarely there; consequently the medical model and the rehabilitation model peaceably coexist, and a non-M.D. democracy prevails in day-to-day treatment." This ambiguous and paradoxical role for the psychiatrist, as both a central and peripheral figure on the team, is common; Pollack and Cutler (1992) refer to this situation as the "giant in the closet." Nevertheless, I think some of this role strain and ambiguity could be improved and that the psychiatrist can have a meaningful, consistent, and well-defined role, not as authoritarian leader but as a senior and respected clinician who shares responsibility for major clinical decisions. The psychiatrist provides direct treatment, oversees treatment plans, and provides biopsychosocial consultation to other team members (Diamond, Stein, and Susser, 1991) but also can share in the treatment team's common effort to form a therapeutic, rehabilitative relationship with the client (Links, Kirkpatrick, and Whelton, 1994). By having coffee with Steven in the community, Mays helped engage the client and also undoubtedly modeled collaborative and creative clinical behavior for other team members. In many programs, psychiatrists also provide much-needed continuity of care, since turnover of case managers may be higher than that of psychiatrists. It is therefore essential that community mental health programs recruit and retain psychiatrists who have meaningful roles and manageable caseloads that permit them to fully participate in the treatment of mentally ill clients (Goldman, Faulkner, and Breeding, 1994).

Commentary References

Coursey, R. D. "Psychotherapy with Persons Suffering from Schizophrenia: The Need for a New Agenda." *Schizophrenia Bulletin,* 1989, *15* (3), 349–353.

Diamond, R. J., Stein, L. I., and Susser, E. "Essential and Nonessential Roles for Psychiatrists in Community Mental Health Centers." *Hospital and Community Psychiatry,* 1991, *42,* 187–189.

Diamond, R. J., and Wikler, D. I. "Ethical Problems in Community Treatment of the Chronically Mentally Ill." In L. I. Stein and M. A. Test (eds.), *The Training in Community Living Model: A Decade of Experience.* New Directions for Mental Health Services, no. 26. San Francisco: Jossey-Bass, 1985.

Drake, R. E., McHugo, G. J., and Noordsy, D. L. "Treatment of Alcoholism Among Schizophrenic Outpatients: Four-Year Outcomes." *American Journal of Psychiatry,* 1993, *150,* 328–329.

Goldman, C. R., Faulkner, L. R., and Breeding, K. A. "Estimating Psychiatrist Staffing Needs in Community Mental Health Programs." *Hospital and Community Psychiatry,* 1994, *45,* 333–337.

Goldman, C. R., Hicks, P. W., Bennett, M., and Leggett, R. P. "Treating Patients with Mental Illness and Chemical Dependency: An Intensive Outpatient Program." *Journal of the South Carolina Medical Association,* 1994, *90* (3), 105–108.

Huxley, P., and Warner, R. "Case Management, Quality of Life, and Satisfaction with Services of Long-Term Psychiatric Patients." *Hospital and Community Psychiatry,* 1992, *43,* 799–802.

Kanter, J. S. "The Process of Change in the Chronic Mentally Ill: A Naturalistic Perspective." *Psychosocial Rehabilitation Journal,* 1985, *9* (1), 55–69.

Kanter, J. S. "Clinical Issues in the Case Management Relationship." In M. Harris and L. Bachrach (eds.), *Clinical Case Management.* New Directions for Mental Health Services, no. 40, San Francisco: Jossey-Bass, 1988.

Lewis, L., and Rosenberg, S. J. "Psychoanalytic Psychotherapy with Brain-Injured Adult Psychiatric Patients. *Journal of Nervous and Mental Disease,* 1990, *178* (2), 69–77.

Links, P. S., Kirkpatrick, H., and Whelton, C. "Psychosocial Rehabilitation and the Role of Psychiatrist." *Psychosocial Rehabilitation Journal,* 1994, *18,* 121–129.

Miller, W. R., and Rollnick, S. *Motivational Interviewing.* New York: Guilford Press, 1991.

Minkoff, K. "Intervention Strategies for Dual Diagnosis." *Innovations and Research,* 1993, *2* (4), 11–17.

Nikkel, R., and Coiner, R. "Critical Interventions and Tasks in Delivering Dual-Diagnosis Services." *Psychosocial Rehabilitation Journal,* 1991, *15* (2), 57–66.

Osher, F. C., and Kofoed, L. L. "Treatment of Patients with Psychiatric and Psychoactive Substance Abuse Disorders." *Hospital and Community Psychiatry,* 1989, *40,* 1025–1030.

Pollack, D. A., and Cutler, D. L. "Psychiatry in Community Mental Health Centers: Everyone Can Win." *Community Mental Health Journal,* 1992, *28,* 259–267.

Prochaska, J. O., DiClemente, C. C., and Norcross, J. C. "In Search of How People Change: Applications to Addictive Behaviors." *American Psychologist,* 1992, *47* (9), 1102–1114.

Schwartz, H. I., Vingiano, W., and Perez, C. B. "Autonomy and the Right to Refuse Treatment: Patients' Attitudes After Involuntary Medication." *Hospital and Community Psychiatry,* 1988, *39,* 1049–1054.

Sokolove, R. L., and Trimble, D. "Assessing Support and Stress in the Social Networks of Chronic Patients." *Hospital and Community Psychiatry,* 1986, *37,* 370–372.

Wasow, M. "The Need for Asylum Revisited." *Hospital and Community Psychiatry,* 1993, *44,* 207–208, 222.

Wasylenki, D. A. "Psychotherapy of Schizophrenia Revisited." *Hospital and Community Psychiatry,* 1992, *43,* 123–127.

Weiden, P., and Havens, L. "Psychotherapeutic Management Techniques in the Treatment of Outpatients with Schizophrenia." *Hospital and Community Psychiatry,* 1994, *45,* 549–555.

Integrating case management, residential services, psychiatric care, and substance abuse treatment, this case report describes a multifaceted treatment approach with a homeless, dually diagnosed client.

Overcoming Crack, Schizophrenia, and Homelessness: A Comprehensive Case Management Approach

John D. Dende, John D. Kline
Commentary by George Hagman

Melvin is a forty-year-old single African-American male diagnosed as paranoid schizophrenic with polysubstance abuse and diabetes. He has a history of multiple hospitalizations for psychosis and substance abuse spanning seventeen years. In this case report, we will be describing how the process of stabilization and recovery proceeded over the course of three and a half years in the dual diagnosis program at Community Connections, a comprehensive inner-city case management agency for severely mentally ill adults that provides psychiatric care, substance abuse treatment, residential opportunities, crisis intervention (including acute hospitalization), psychotherapy, and vocational programs (Harris and Bergman, 1987; Kline, Harris, Bebout, and Drake, 1991).

Melvin was born in a poor neighborhood in New York City, the eldest of three boys. His father was a truck driver, on the road for weeks, home for only a few days at a time. During his brief visits to the home, he was authoritarian and physically abusive, often drunk, and inept around children. Melvin recalls, "He would spank us for not listening and spank us if we listened but didn't do things right."

Melvin's homelife was chaotic. When he was ten, three boys were virtually deposited on his family's doorstep—his teenage half-brothers from a previous marriage his mother never mentioned. Within the first year of their stay, two half-brothers were sent to a juvenile detention center, one for his fire-setting, another for assault and robbery. When Melvin was twelve, his father was imprisoned for murder, but Melvin was told that his father went off with another woman. At this point, the family moved to Melvin's grandfather's house, a period he described as horrible and restricting.

Melvin's mother was debilitated both physically and emotionally. Though he sometimes describes his mother in glowing terms—"a happy, humorous, resourceful woman"—he also describes her as helpless and depressed. During his early teens, his mother became increasingly incapacitated, and Melvin assumed considerable household responsibility. When Melvin was fifteen, his mother died suddenly. The children were placed with an aunt whose husband was violent and alcoholic. Melvin began using alcohol, marijuana, and LSD.

At seventeen, Melvin joined the Marines and was stationed overseas, becoming addicted to opium toward the end of his tour. He went AWOL several times but was honorably discharged. He returned to Washington, D.C., and took a job driving a delivery truck. He lived in his stepmother's boarding house with his half-sister, a cocaine user. He started some occasional cocaine use but mostly continued to abuse alcohol.

Melvin's father, now released from prison, also lived at this boarding house. His father was critical, often demanding extra money and chores from Melvin. One day, Melvin came home and started hearing "voices." He went out back and started kicking and smashing his father's broken car. Later, he began hearing voices telling him he was evil, to kill himself, and to go back to New York. He was involuntarily committed and started on antipsychotic medication.

During the next ten years, Melvin was repeatedly hospitalized for psychotic symptoms that were exacerbated by his continuing abuse of alcohol, marijuana, and cocaine. During these hospitalizations, he received no addiction treatment and was told to go to Alcoholics Anonymous (AA) meetings. He attended several meetings but did not find them helpful. Unemployed, he used SSI and VA disability to support himself.

In 1987, Melvin was admitted to the dual diagnosis unit at the local VA hospital. At this unit, he finally began to learn about mental illness and substance abuse and began an ongoing relationship with Dr. A., a psychiatrist he describes as "like a father to me." Despite the positive effects of this relationship, he continued a pattern of medication noncompliance, drug use, and frequent rehospitalization over the next four years. Finally, three and a half years ago, Melvin was referred by the VA dual diagnosis unit to Community Connections for intensive case management.

I (Dende) first met Melvin on the dual diagnosis ward where he had been an inpatient for nine months. We were introduced by his psychiatrist and the unit social worker. He immediately requested assistance in finding stable housing. I told him we operated subsidized, abstinence-oriented housing. If residents use drugs, we send them to detoxification units before they can return to their apartments or group homes. I asked him if he could make a commitment to an abstinent lifestyle and accept this condition. If he was not interested in abstinence-oriented housing, we could help him locate unsubsidized and poorer quality housing that was not accountable to the agency.

Since finding decent housing seemed important to Melvin, I asked him about prior housing experiences as part of a rapport-building assessment. He told me that he did poorly in unstructured living arrangements such as apartments and did better with more structured situations, such as the military or a staffed group home. Commenting that "you seem to be more stable at places where there are some expectations and other people around to talk to," I introduced the option of placement in our group home, a temporary transitional residence used primarily for evaluation purposes.

We agreed to meet twice weekly at the hospital for a month before his discharge. During this time, we could help him identify his goals and negotiate a community treatment plan.

From the outset, I was assessing Melvin's ability to form an alliance with me. He seemed likeable, friendly, and eager to say the right things with some sincerity: "I want to stay off crack cocaine and attend your Relapse Prevention groups." In our initial meeting, he looked for approval from the ward psychiatrist and social worker, suggesting a capacity to form a therapeutic alliance.

To help motivate Melvin toward an abstinent lifestyle, I began working with him immediately on identifying the negative consequences of his past substance use. These included homelessness, loss of jobs, loss of friends, paranoia, diabetic crises, delusions, hallucinations, angry outbursts, increased depression, risk of incarceration, poor hygiene, impoverishment, and guilt over his stealing from his friends and family. In the weeks to come, we would repeatedly review these consequences so they would become automatic responses when he developed a craving. I also helped him describe these cravings so he could identify them quickly and use alternative strategies.

However, even before his discharge, we disagreed on the need to allow the agency to become payee for his VA disability benefits. In the hospital, Melvin had been depositing his money in a hospital account monitored by staff. Previously, in the community, he received his check himself and usually spent it quickly on crack, often becoming homeless or rehospitalized. Though he trusted the ward psychiatrist and social worker with his money, he was reluctant to trust me. Despite encouragement from the ward staff, Melvin only agreed to make the agency payee because it was a condition of discharge. During his nine-month hospitalization, he saved over $3,000. He hesitantly signed over these funds to the agency's client account and was promised a monthly accounting of his funds. He then wanted $100 weekly in spending money. Despite Melvin's insistence that he no longer craved cocaine, I feared that such an amount would tempt him to use. I persuaded Melvin to accept $50 weekly with incremental increases as abstinence was sustained. If he used cocaine, his weekly allotment would drop by $25, which could be earned back in $5 weekly increments for each week of clean urine.

In our predischarge meetings, Melvin and I frequently discussed this issue of money management. He stated that "you are going to take my money and use it for yourself" and that "you can't trust anyone, especially with your money." He believed that his grandfather agreed to care for him and his brothers "only because of the welfare checks." His family often asked him for money, and he tried to buy their approval and support.

In the weeks before discharge, I often took Melvin out on passes. I used these opportunities to observe him in community settings and we would discuss his views of life outside the protection of the hospital. He seemed to look forward to my visits and seemed interested in collaborating in treatment. He said all the right things: that he wanted to continue Haldol because it "really helps me with the voices and I need it," that he wanted "to stay off drugs because they mess up my life," that he wanted to "give myself insulin regularly because it helps avoid medical crises," and that he wanted "to do more with my life, maybe get a job or volunteer somewhere." Although I was aware that his situation was much more complicated, these were encouraging words. We often discussed relapse prevention. I asked Melvin to imagine life outside the hospital and how he would avoid substance abuse. I used a metaphor of the collaborative scientist—that we would collect evidence on improving his success at achieving his goals, revising the treatment plan to solve problems on our journey. As he became more comfortable with me, he agreed to take three drug screens a week, to appoint the agency as payee, and to begin a volunteer job at the hospital three days a week. He also agreed to attend the agency substance abuse groups as well as Narcotics Anonymous groups at the hospital.

After discharge from the hospital, Melvin settled in well at the crisis house. With his affable and outgoing manner, he was well liked by staff and residents and was one of the few residents who offered to help with chores. I visited the house a few times a week, and we frequently discussed substance abuse issues. I repeatedly suggested that addiction is a problem mistaken for a solution and that we were going to work on alternative solutions. I acknowledged that cocaine temporarily made him feel good and less lonely. I also helped him recognize that crack use ultimately exacerbated his loneliness because people ignored him when he had no money.

The first crisis in our relationship occurred when Melvin began "cheeking" his Haldol. House staff quickly noticed this when they found him up at 3 A.M. and reported it to me. He also was more withdrawn and had missed a day of volunteer work. Melvin said he stopped the medicine because he was feeling "too lazy" and was embarrassed by periodic facial grimacing and hand tremors that he believed diminished his sexual attractiveness. Yet he also recognized that the medicine helped keep the voices away. We discussed the pros and cons of medication use, then made an appointment to see the agency psychiatrist. I had prepared the psychiatrist and suggested that he emphasize that injectable medications sometimes reduce side effects. After some discussion, Melvin agreed to begin injections of an antipsychotic medication.

After six weeks at the crisis house, Melvin moved to a less-structured group home that was not operated by Community Connections. Though I would have preferred placing Melvin in an agency group home with better-trained staff, Community Connections facilities had no beds available. The new house was located near the neighborhood where his stepmother's boarding house was. Melvin preferred this area because of the familiar surroundings, but I was concerned that he would resume relationships with drug users and dealers. When I would drive him home, he was often delighted when he recognized old acquaintances on the street corners. When he acknowledged that he used drugs with them, we discussed methods for coping with these temptations including travel routes that would avoid them. We also role-played methods to refuse offers of drugs.

Melvin acknowledged that these street-corner acquaintances helped alleviate his loneliness and bolster his fragile sense of identity. While respecting these needs, I attempted to help him become aware of the risks of these associations. I often questioned him, in Socratic fashion, about whether these "friends" would welcome him if he was not involved in drugs. He acknowledged that they would likely reject him if he told them he no longer used drugs. When we would pass people on the street that he knew, I would jokingly ask him if that was a "friend" or a "user." After repeating this distinction, he stopped calling these people friends.

During this period, I referred Melvin to our agency's substance abuse groups. Melvin joined a discussion group on problems of living and an education group on substance abuse. I co-lead these groups, and I used this dual role to encourage his participation and enhance my understanding of him. He also viewed these groups as an opportunity for further contact with me.

About two months later, Melvin's ex-girlfriend, a prostitute, visited him at the new group home and offered to sell him crack cocaine. He saved his $10-a-day spending money until he had $30 and then paid her for sex. He said he refused cocaine the first few times, but she refused to have sex with him unless he also smoked some. He eventually acquiesced and then asked me for funds to buy a new Walkman. His impatient and demanding demeanor alerted me to the possibility of relapse, and I asked him to cooperate with a urine screen.

Awaiting the results of the urine screen and unaware of his contacts with his ex-girlfriend, I gave Melvin the money he requested, though I was concerned about signs of stress and his recent avoidance of me. When I pointed out these changes, he denied any difficulties and seemed vindicated when his urine screen was negative. Unfortunately, this lab result was probably erroneous. He stole $1,300 worth of TVs and VCRs from the group home in the next two weeks. I tracked him down at the group home and learned that he had been using crack regularly with his ex-girlfriend. He was remorseful and agreed to replace the items with his savings. I was quite disturbed by this criminal act but persuaded the group home staff and clients not to press legal charges because he planned to make prompt restitution. I feared that jail would injure this genuinely remorseful client. However, I told him that charges would be pressed if it happened again. (In subsequent relapses, he sold only his own possessions.)

After Melvin spent a few days at a detox facility, I joined him and his housemates on a shopping trip to the electronics store. As he repurchased the stolen items, we all talked about how it felt to have items stolen. Melvin apologized to his housemates and informed them about his problems with cocaine use.

Melvin became very guilty and depressed after this episode, and I feared that the intensity of his self-blame might lead to further use. To counteract this tendency and bolster his self-esteem, I repeatedly emphasized that the "real" Melvin was a competent, functional person who could save his money to buy desired possessions and could earn the trust and affection of others. This helped him to deflect blame for the relapse away from himself and allowed him to focus on the uncomfortable feelings—loneliness and depression—that lead him to seek relief in drugs.

For the next six months, Melvin remained abstinent and continued his three-day-a-week volunteer work along with group therapy three times a week. He began to form relationships with group members and was admired by his peers, often volunteering to share how he coped with drug cravings. In these sessions, he often referred to advice I had given him, indicating that he would think of what I would say or do in the same situation.

During this period of abstinence, Melvin moved precipitously to a supervised, independent apartment. This occurred ten months after his discharge from the hospital. At the group home, the resident manager had become involved in several altercations with friends, and we had to transfer all our clients. Melvin initially denied that these altercations bothered him but later admitted that they evoked frightening childhood memories.

While placed temporarily at our crisis house, Melvin began asking for his own apartment. Since he met the criteria for independent living (six months abstinence, a daily activity, homemaking skills, and an ability to self-administer medications and monitor his diabetes), our team agreed to a trial placement in his own apartment with a strict contract regarding urine screens and glucose levels. Melvin managed in his apartment for two months but started complaining about feeling lonely. Although he was in a building with other agency clients, they were not very sociable. Lonely and isolated, he started visiting his ex-girlfriend. His medication compliance and his attendance at his volunteer work became more erratic.

During one of the days Melvin missed work at the hospital, Dr. A. suddenly died of a heart attack. Melvin became quite distraught at this loss. He went on a cocaine binge, and became psychotic. Physically depleted from drug use and missing several insulin shots, he admitted himself to the hospital and was treated in the intensive care unit for several days. He blamed himself for his psychiatrist's death and insisted that he could have saved Dr. A.'s life had he been working at the hospital. "I know I could have rushed him down to the operating room in time," he said.

I visited Melvin in the hospital and worked with the hospital staff to help Melvin grieve for this loss. He also began talking about the sudden death of his mother when he was fifteen. Instead of adequately mourning this childhood loss, he had begun to heavily use alcohol and drugs. Now, with adequate support, he discovered he could bear this grief without substance use.

We discussed this relapse episode in considerable detail, role-playing ways to refuse offers of drugs from his ex-girlfriend. Thereafter, I routinely inquired whether she was visiting and helped him recognize that the pleasure of their contacts was soon followed by intense feelings of abandonment when his funds were depleted. This relapse episode and subsequent reparative mourning experience significantly increased Melvin's commitment to treatment and abstinence. I no longer had to persuade Melvin of the wisdom of abstinence; the content of our discussions now focused on how to change, not whether to change. As part of an overall strategy for maintaining abstinence, Melvin was willing to move from his own apartment to a structured group home. He would often say, "I need to be put in a box"—his metaphor for the "holding" environment he desperately needed. At the agency group home, he enjoyed the companionship of staff and residents, had his medications and insulin monitored, and kept a curfew. He insisted on taking urine screens five days a week because he said he did not trust himself. He envisioned this self-imposed monitoring as one plank in his box; others included money management, daily volunteer work at the hospital, weekly Haldol injections, and dual diagnosis therapy groups.

Our staff at this group home were more highly trained than the staff at his previous house. They would let Melvin talk about his urges to use crack while reinforcing the simple coping strategies written into his treatment plan—holding his money, giving him a chore, or reviewing selected self-statements that could help him relax.

Again, he took initiative in performing chores that elicited much appreciation. This enhanced his self-esteem and distracted him from his urges to use. He also adopted a "big brother" role with some less functional clients and began to proudly identify Community Connections as a surrogate family. Melvin became particularly fond of one residential staff member who helped transport him to a detox facility during another relapse. Over time, he came to trust the staff and would tell them promptly when he had used drugs. Because of this involvement and my ongoing communication with the house staff, I was able to reduce my contact with Melvin to three times a week.

Six months after moving to this group home (and eighteen months after referral to our agency), Melvin decided to return to competitive employment to reduce idle time and to accumulate money for future needs. I helped him obtain an evening shift position microfilming records on a military base. This schedule was chosen to minimize opportunities for relapse and enable him to attend group therapy. On the job, Melvin told his supervisors that he was a cocaine user and that if he started missing work or looked tired they should call his case manager. Since he was still not confident he would be able to self-report his use, he requested others in his support network to monitor any signs of relapse.

During this period, Melvin's dependent attachment to me became more evident. I learned that he feared relapse because he worried that I would abandon him if this occurred. Similarly, when I traveled to Toronto for a conference, he worried that the agency was opening a Toronto office and that I would be transferred. He also expressed concern about the mechanical condition of my car and offered to buy me a new one. As this attachment developed, he would go out of his way to ensure my continued support. For example, when I began reducing my control over his finances, he insisted on showing me the receipts for everything he spent. This suggested that he had so little confidence in his inner controls that he wanted me involved—in reality and fantasy—in sustaining external controls.

During this active-treatment phase, I helped Melvin become more assertive with his exploitative relatives. He felt guilty about not helping them out but resented their increasing requests. With a job, a partial VA disability pension, and subsidized housing, he sometimes had extra funds. He would sometimes give his family members so much money that he was unable to meet his own needs. In a family meeting, Melvin, with much rehearsal, told them that he would no longer give or loan them money, especially since his father was actively alcoholic and his sister was using crack. As he became more confident of the stability of his new support networks, he was more comfortable resisting his family's demands as he was less afraid of losing their erratic support.

Three years after entering our program, Melvin continued to progress. He had attained seven months of abstinence, continued to live successfully in the group home, worked competitively for three months, and begun a relationship with a non-substance-abusing woman who was also an agency client. At this point, as he moved from an "active treatment" to a "relapse prevention" phase (Osher and Kofoed, 1989), Melvin felt confident enough to request a move to a more independent living situation. As he did not want to live alone, he was interested in a room in an agency-run house with four other abstinent clients that had no on-site supervision other than a weekly meeting. This home provided an opportunity for both privacy and socializing in an abstinent environment, the residents being invested in keeping a sober house. As Melvin was attached to the staff at his former group home, he was encouraged to participate in that home's recreational activities. Similarly, he continued to visit the VA hospital where he had been a patient and a volunteer.

Melvin's job continued to be an important source of self-esteem. Each day, he arrived an hour early at the van pickup area. He rapidly advanced on the job but began to experience more drug cravings. Before using, he reported these to me. He also told me how he was coping with these urges, including hiding his money and talking to his housemates.

This phase of treatment has provided new challenges for Melvin. For instance, though he started to feel bored by his job's repetitive tasks, he was afraid to tell his supervisor because he thought the supervisor would be disappointed and angry. He asked me to call the supervisor and advocate for him. Instead, we rehearsed ways he could negotiate with his supervisor. Melvin reported back that he had negotiated a job rotation schedule. He was surprised that his supervisor seemed appreciative of his assertiveness. Thereafter, when Melvin expressed doubts about his competence or social skills, I reminded him of how well he handled this situation.

The progress that Melvin has made during three and a half years of dual diagnosis treatment is evidence of the changes homeless, dual diagnosis adults can make in their lives when given adequate support and treatment. Currently, Melvin plans to marry his girlfriend and, if all goes well, share an apartment with her. He continues to excel on his job and manage his relapse-prevention program responsibly. Melvin's movement through the stages of treatment has not been linear or steady. There have been setbacks and relapses, and Melvin's commitment to treatment has often wavered. But by remaining consistently supportive and reframing his relapses as opportunities to learn, we were able to help him benefit from the comprehensive dual diagnosis program at Community Connections.

Discussion

Melvin's story illustrates an integrated, comprehensive case management approach to assisting homeless, dual diagnosis adults achieve psychiatric stability and community reintegration (Kline, Harris, Bebout, and Drake, 1991; Drake and others, 1993). To achieve these goals, these clients require aggressive intervention, with intensive levels of support and structure, which is gradually reduced as stabilization and recovery progress. The essential elements of the process include the case management relationship, the continuum of housing opportunities, the structure and containment provided for the individual client, and dual diagnosis group treatment. In this discussion, I will briefly examine how each of these elements contributed to Melvin's recovery.

The Case Management Relationship. The multifaceted intervention in this case report required a strong foundation in the relationship between Melvin and his case manager. This relationship illustrates four characteristics that are essential when treating homeless, dual diagnosis clients: optimism, patience, flexibility, and assertiveness.

Case managers must remain *optimistic,* despite frequent setbacks, about clients' capacities to improve their lives. In Melvin's case, over three years of intensive work were required to move from a life of crack addiction, psychosis, and homelessness to an abstinent lifestyle in the community. By remaining optimistic, the case manager provided Melvin with support and encouragement that arrested the circular process of addiction, relapse, and recidivism before Melvin lost faith in the treatment process.

Besides the optimism needed to invest time and energy in clients, case managers also need the *patience* to persevere in providing consistent, effective treatment over long periods of time. Clients have impaired ego functioning— poor impulse control, inadequate coping skills, and poor judgment—that leads them to alternate between desperate efforts to resolve their problems immediately and paralyzing bouts of despair and demoralization. Case managers learn to understand these impairments, recognizing that any of them may derail the treatment process.

In Melvin's case, his development of relapse-prevention skills was a slow process. Although he had considerable skill at independent living and responded well to medication, his crack use would deplete his finances, undermine his psychotropic medications, increase his risk of diabetic complications, and severely undermine his commitment to treatment. Over time, Melvin began to internalize his case manager's patient responses to each setback, learning to replace the cocaine user's craving for excitement and euphoria with a capacity to tolerate disappointment, frustration, and loss (Harris and Bergman, 1987).

Case managers must also remain *flexible* and creative in finding the combination of interventions that works best for each client. During Melvin's involvement with our program, the case manager assisted with five residential transitions, sometimes on short notice, in response to Melvin's wishes and capacities and to changing environmental circumstances.

Finally, case managers must be *assertive* with these clients. At times, they must assertively discuss the consequences of substance abuse and persuade their clients to accept the structure and containment needed to maintain abstinence. In this case, the case manager persisted in this assertive position, well aware that it would often evoke anger and resistance.

Structure and Containment. As this report illustrates, homeless, dual diagnosis adults often benefit from a case management approach involving structure and containment. This approach helps clients, particularly in the early stages of treatment, contain impulses to abuse substances and engage in other destructive acting out. In Melvin's case, these interventions included money management, random urinalysis, a group home curfew, and an evening job. These interventions were essential components of the "box" that helped Melvin control his behavior.

In Melvin's case, money management was the central element in containing his impulses to use cocaine. As noted, the agency became the representative payee for his VA disability and the case manager closely monitored his finances. While we at Community Connections support the goal of client self-determination, we believe there are compelling reasons to use such methods with homeless, dual diagnosis clients, especially with those struggling with the powerful influence of crack cocaine. The unique addictive mechanisms of this drug are very destructive. The very sudden peak psychoactive effect and the very abbreviated high leaves the user immediately depleted and desperately seeking more crack. Frequently, users will only stop using the substance when all funds are depleted and they are homeless. Money management is a valuable tool for modulating these impulsive attempts to procure crack, giving the client an opportunity to experience longer periods of breathing space without the drug.

When Melvin was first referred to Community Connections, he had been using crack for ten years, his only periods of abstinence coming during his frequent inpatient stays. If Melvin had prevailed when he was discharged from the VA hospital, he would have kept control of his funds and likely continued his ten-year pattern of crack abuse, homelessness, and hospitalization, increasing his risk for medical complications or imprisonment.

Also, during the early phases of recovery from crack abuse, clients must learn relapse-prevention skills to identify and manage stimulus cues that trigger powerful urges for crack. Many clients think of crack as soon as they see their disability checks or any other money. Money management removes this potent stimulus for usage, giving clients time to develop the skills and support needed to regain control of their personal finances.

Returning clients to financial autonomy is a trial-and-error process that requires much clinical skill (Brotman and Miller, 1990). As Melvin abstained from drugs, the case manager would increase his weekly stipend. Over time, Melvin was able to carry larger and larger sums of money without succumbing to his cravings for crack.

Other interventions also augmented these functions. Random urinalysis reduced Melvin's opportunities to use without the knowledge of the agency. The group home curfew took him off the street during the hours when he would be most vulnerable to relapse. Similarly, when choosing a job, the case manager and Melvin agreed that the evening shift would have the same effect of occupying his time during high-risk evening hours. These interventions clearly helped to reduce the frequency, severity, and duration of relapse.

The Housing Continuum. Community Connections offers a continuum of housing options for homeless, dual diagnosis clients—highly structured group homes, closely supervised "training" apartments, and lightly supervised independent apartments. Homeless, dual diagnosis clients present special challenges to this housing continuum. The agency housing available to clients is dependent on their commitment to abstinence and progress in dual diagnosis treatment.

If a client is actively abusing at the time of referral, the agency will always choose a structured, abstinence-oriented group home. There are several reasons for this policy. First, the aforementioned dynamics of crack addiction are so powerful that there is little chance of a successful transition from drug abuse and homelessness to independent living without intervening housing support. At one point early in our work with dual diagnosis clients, Community Connections offered independent apartments to crack abusers who claimed they had stopped using. These were clients who had agreed to a program of money management with the agency. Within one month, the building of these clients was taken over by drug dealers. Our clients were using and distributing crack out of this building and, when funds were depleted, prostituting themselves to obtain more.

Second, many clients, though maintaining a tenuous abstinence, are vulnerable to the influence of their prior social networks of drug abusers. Structured group housing gives such clients more support for resisting the influence of these former associates, partly by reducing the opportunities for contact with other users and partly by facilitating the development of drug-free networks. Third, structured housing gives agency staff more opportunity to monitor treatment compliance. The group home environment allows us to reinforce our expectations for abstinence through urine screens and psychotropic medication.

Finally, as noted, all residents are endangered when fellow clients use or deal drugs, engage in related criminal activity, or associate with active users or dealers. Dealers and prostitutes will harass other building residents for money or shelter, intimidating them into acquiescence and silence. Also, such activity would elicit cries of alarm from neighbors, who would oppose any future housing initiatives by our agency. The level of housing support necessary for maintaining abstinence varies with each client. As Melvin's experience illustrates, clients move from more structured to more independent housing as they progress. Melvin moved, with several detours, from crisis house to supervised group home to independent group residence in three years as the stability of his abstinence developed.

Regardless of the quality of housing or clinical treatment, homeless, dual diagnosis clients often relapse. Unless programs have workable plans for addressing these setbacks, formerly homeless clients will be returned to the streets. Other than insisting on a brief stay in a detoxification program, Community Connections does not mandate any particular response to relapse or any specific limit to the frequency of these setbacks. Our policy empowers the case manager and other agency staff to negotiate a response to the relapse with the client. This policy attempts to balance the need for safe living environments for all clients with tolerance and flexibility toward previously homeless, relapse-prone residents.

Group Treatment. Community Connections also offers a range of substance-abuse treatment groups for homeless, dual diagnosis adults (Noordsy and Fox, 1991). At different times during Melvin's treatment, he attended all of these groups. For clients in the early stages of treatment, we offer the Problems of Living discussion group and a psychoeducation group. Both groups are designed to accommodate clients who are currently using substances and are ambivalent about abstinence. Adapted for psychotic clients, both groups offer an empathic, nonconfrontational climate that carefully regulates the level of affect stimulation (Miller and Rollnick, 1991). These groups provide a safe milieu for clients to discuss their problems of daily life, listen to the experiences of other homeless adults, and exchange information on the consequences of substance abuse.

Specifically, the Problems of Living group is designed to elicit an open-ended discussion of client concerns such as jobs, family, housing, and finances. Although these groups are not explicitly educational, the leaders often identify substance abuse as a precipitant of many problems of living. More explicitly didactic, the psychoeducation groups include films and structured discussions covering three topics: mental illness, substance use, and homelessness.

For clients in the later stages of treatment and committed to an abstinent lifestyle, we offer a social skills training group that emphasizes maintaining relapse prevention through behavioral rehearsal of coping strategies, cognitive reframing, methods for stress reduction, and communication skills.

Melvin illustrates a successful outcome of dual diagnosis treatment at Community Connections. He is abstinent from drugs, in independent housing, psychiatrically stable, and successfully employed. During the past three and a half years, the case manager always maintained a long-term goal of promoting Melvin's independence and autonomy. To achieve this end, our interventions contained some coercive and controlling elements including money management, urine screening, and mandatory placement in a structured group home.

These interventions appear to challenge important principles of mental health service, particularly those of consumer choice, empowerment, and self-determination. However, our experience has demonstrated that temporary restrictions on client autonomy are sometimes needed to attain a lifestyle of health, stability, and independence. As case managers, we must sometimes strongly advocate for the temporary implementation of such measures. Without such interventions, homeless, dual diagnosis adults may continue in a destructive cycle of drug use, homelessness, and hospitalization. However, as Melvin's story illustrates, even the most troubled residents of our streets can resume lives of dignity, security, and respect with the help of a comprehensive case management approach.

References

Brotman, A., and Miller, W. "The Therapist as Representative Payee." *Hospital and Community Psychiatry,* 1990, *41,* 167–171.

Drake, R. E., Bartels, S. J., Teague, G. B., Noordsy, D. L., and Clark, R. E. "Treatment of Substance Abuse in Severely Mentally Ill Patients." *Journal of Nervous and Mental Disorders,* 1993, *181* (10), 606–611.

Harris, M., and Bergman, H. C. "Case Management with the Chronically Mentally Ill: A Clinical Perspective." *American Journal of Orthopsychiatry,* 1987, *57* (2), 296–302.

Kline, J., Harris, M., Bebout, R. R., and Drake, R. E., "Contrasting Integrated and Linkage Models of Treatment for Homeless, Dually Diagnosed Adults." In K. Minkoff and R. E. Drake (eds.), *Dual Diagnosis of Major Mental Illness and Substance Disorder.* New Directions for Mental Health Services, no. 50. San Francisco: Jossey-Bass, 1991.

Miller, W. R., and Rollnick, S. *Motivational Interviewing.* New York: Guilford Press, 1991.

Noordsy, D. L., and Fox, L. "Group Intervention Techniques for People with Dual Disorders." *Psychosocial Rehabilitation Journal,* 1991, *15,* 67–78.

Osher, F. C., and Kofoed, L. L. "Treatment of Patients with Psychiatric and Psychoactive Substance Abuse Disorders." *Hospital and Community Psychiatry,* 1989, *40,* 1025–1030.

John D. Dende, M.A., is clinical coordinator of the independent apartment program at Community Connections in Washington, D.C.

John D. Kline, M.S.W., is program director of the dual diagnosis program at Community Connections in Washington, D.C.

Commentary

George Hagman, C.S.W.
Clinical Director, Substance Abuse Treatment Program
Montefiore Medical Center, New York

As a clinical social worker who has provided case management to severely mentally ill clients on Manhattan's Lower East Side for eight years, I found much to admire in Dende and Kline's report of their work with Melvin, a drug-addicted, mentally ill man: the forging of a stable treatment alliance; Dende's effectiveness in providing structure and containment over time; and ultimately the indisputable success in helping Melvin achieve a better life. Recognizing these achievements, my comments will focus on the implications of using an aggressive, highly structured management approach and on the dynamics of the helping relationship in work with dually diagnosed clients.

In their discussion, Dende and Kline explain their rationale that dually disordered clients (especially crack abusers) need considerable structuring and containment to achieve a successful outcome. From this viewpoint, if Melvin had control of his money, relapse would have been almost inevitable. They state that money management is a valuable method for modulating these impulsive attempts to procure crack by giving the client an opportunity to experience longer periods of breathing space without the drug. In addition, the drug-free residential services at Community Connections required Melvin and other residents to agree to close monitoring of their abstinence.

Recognizing Melvin's impressive recovery, this approach prompted me to consider several important clinical issues. First, would similar aggressive interventions work with less compliant or submissive clients? Many dually diagnosed clients are intractable, especially those most in need. In spite of blatant disability, these clients may hold fast to their (often illusory) autonomy and recoil from such conditional offers of help.

For example, one of my clients would initially sit and listen as I laid out the terms of my brilliantly conceived treatment plan. When I stopped talking, he would smile politely and said, "No, thank you." During a trip to the welfare office on the day of his hospital discharge, he gave me the slip and disappeared for weeks. The ease with which Melvin's initial contract was developed (with assistance from the heavy hand of the VA) does not speak to the problem of engaging more reluctant clients. To be sure, there are many clients as submissive and cooperative as Melvin, but many might never comply with Dende's conditions and interventions.

Second, under what circumstances are we as care providers justified in coercing (however benignly) such clearly self-defeating persons to cooperate with our service efforts? Dende and Kline suggest that the end justifies the means, citing Melvin's functional and psychiatric rehabilitation from mental illness and social impairment. Case managers need to consider several questions before deciding whether to adopt this approach: Does the funding come from a public agency with a mandate to serve all eligible clients within a catchment area, or from a private agency with more a limited, conditional mandate? (A private agency can be more assertive because it can use public agencies as a safety net.) How extensive is the obligation to assure a drug-free safe environment for other agency clients? Would a less structured, noncoercive approach offer therapeutic possibilities that would eventually reduce the client's apparent risks?

Dende and Kline illustrated how Melvin did better with more structure and containment, but others might still argue that clients should be free to make whatever decisions they wish if they are not in imminent danger. These are important questions for which there are no easy answers.

In contrast to the strategies used in Melvin's case, my own case management approach with homeless, dually diagnosed clients has been an unconditional one, largely free of coercive interventions. Admittedly, I usually had no other option. The agency where I worked was an independent clinical case management team without its own residential programs. As a result, we were unable to offer any tangible support beyond our personal and case management skills. Since our program had been established to engage noncompliant clients, we had to develop voluntary alliances and service agreements even when we believed that these plans were inadequate. Our primary goal was to establish a helping relationship with persons who had fallen through the cracks. We understood our role as just "being there," available on a daily basis to be used by the clients for psychological support or to help them obtain environmental resources. During times of danger, we took stronger measures, including involuntary inpatient admissions. However, in general, we negotiated mutually agreeable, but often limited, service plans.

Interestingly, we found that many dually diagnosed clients responded well to this approach. Our unconditional acceptance provided them with security from coercion, which many resistant (and even paranoid) clients need. As a working alliance developed, we would also adopt the motivational interviewing approach, focusing our counseling on the client's ambivalence, using the strength of our working alliance to tip the scale of indecision toward change (Miller and Rollnick, 1991).

I came to believe that we were offering our clients one of the only opportunities available in New York City's chaotic social welfare system to get help *without* conditions or negative consequences. In fact, we supported them over many years as they struggled to cope with the many conditions, restrictions, and coercions that plagued their lives. The focus of much of our work involved working with clients in negotiating and enduring these difficult demands.

Over time, I came to believe that treatment efforts, coercive or noncoercive, are successful only when there is a relationship that the client experiences as empathic and supportive. In any case, case managers must remain alert to the dilemma of control versus autonomy in their day-to-day work with clients so as not to fall too readily into one position or the other. On the one hand, rigid adherence to issues of consumerism and empowerment can prevent us from providing the structure and containment that many clients need; on the other hand, the too-ready use of conditions and controls can lead to abuse of authority and to coercion masquerading as care and concern.

A third and related issue is the dynamics of the multiple interpersonal dimensions of the case management relationship (Kanter, 1988). At different points in time, the relationship between case manager and client may resemble the relationship between parent and child (at various developmental levels), siblings, friends, teacher and student, and doctor and patient. Each of these configurations is characterized by a different *mode of relatedness*. For example:

Dependence, as on parents for environmental support
Reliance, as on a parent for emotional support in coping with anxiety, frustration, mourning, and other emotions
Rivalry, as of siblings
Pleasurable mutuality, as in friendship
Didactic interaction, as in teaching
Expert care, as in doctoring

At times, the case management relationship reflects all of these ways of relating, yet we eventually hope to see a progression from the more dependent and didactic modes toward increasing mutuality and client self-efficacy.

Dende and Kline's depiction of the relationship with Melvin seems somewhat one-dimensional, relying on the more parental and didactic modes of relating. The report conveys an authoritarian tone to Dende's interventions, and a submissive quality to Melvin's responses (a characteristic noted by Dende in his initial contact with Melvin). Although the report highlights Melvin's dependance on Dende—noting Melvin's expressed fear of losing him if he used drugs—I am convinced that there were other dimensions to their relationship, and I strongly suspect that Dende greatly enjoyed Melvin's charm, helpfulness, and commitment to recovery.

Perhaps the didactic and somewhat authoritarian tone of this report reflects the influence of the psychoeducational approaches that dominate the clinical literature on teaching substance-abusing, dual diagnosis clients (Drake and others, 1993; Osher and Kofoed, 1989). These approaches highlight the centrality of persuasion in the treatment process. Following this model, Dende aggressively reeducates Melvin on how to abstain from drugs and live a better life—and he is very successful. However, I think the report would have been strengthened if it had explicitly described the more affiliative aspects of the relationship—humor, play, hanging out—that are not evident in the case narrative. Unless clients like Melvin feel liked, admired, and even loved by their case managers, no amount of structure or social resources will suffice.

To some extent, society's negative attitude toward *dependency*—represented in our field by many programs that have "independence" in their titles—makes it hard to see the positive, sustaining and empowering role that healthy *attachments* have in our lives and in the lives of our clients. But if greater autonomy and self-efficacy are the goals of our interventions, then how do we understand the role of a fundamentally dependent attachment in the achievement of these goals? I have found in my own work that more often than not positive attachment does not interfere but continues to provide essential support that, in turn, enhances the client's capacity to adapt and to maintain hard-won gains. The key issue is the management of the client's attachment and the eventual fate of any submissive elements in the relationship. Thus, an important challenge for Melvin and his case manager in the coming years will be the transition from a psychoeducational role into a more classic position of therapeutic neutrality.

In closing, I believe that the case report implicitly demonstrates not so much the curative power of structure and containment as the force of mutual, passionate human involvement. Quite possibly Melvin had never encountered a person like Dende. Of course, he initially feared and was suspicious of Dende's intentions. What models did he have? Poor ones, to be sure. Gradually, incrementally, a relationship was forged between these two men. Was it Dende's hold on the purse strings that encouraged Melvin to change? At least this provided a reason to remain in regular contact. Was it Dende's dogged attention to Melvin's addiction and his use of motivational interviewing techniques? Perhaps. Was it the Community Connections continuum of housing alternatives that offered a series of "holding environments" as Melvin progressed? Certainly a critical factor. But most importantly, Melvin experienced how Dende was *simply there,* willing to attend to his evolving needs and travails, struggling with him, and surviving over time. That is what ultimately matters the most, is it not? Persistence, acceptance, empathy, honesty, simple availability, and helpfulness.

Commentary References

Drake, R. E., Bartels, S. J., Teague, G. B., Noordsy, D. L., and Clark, R. E. "Treatment of Substance Abuse in Severely Mentally Ill Patients." *Journal of Nervous and Mental Disorders,* 1993, *181* (10), 606–611.

Kanter, J. S. "Clinical Issues in the Case Management Relationship." In M. Harris and L. Bachrach (eds.), *Clinical Case Management.* New Directions for Mental Health Services, no. 40. San Francisco: Jossey-Bass, 1988.

Miller, W. R., and Rollnick, S. *Motivational Interviewing.* New York: Guilford Press, 1991.

Osher, F. C., and Kofoed, L. L. "Treatment of Patients with Psychiatric and Psychoactive Substance Abuse Disorders." *Hospital and Community Psychiatry,* 1989, *40,* 1025–1030.

This case report describes the challenges of addressing issues of childhood trauma and integrating psychotherapeutic and environmental interventions when community treatment is interrupted by frequent rehospitalizations.

Sexual Abuse, Suicidality, and Survival: A Clinical Case Management Approach

Joseph Walsh
Commentary by Maxine Harris

In November, 1985, a colleague at Marwood Counseling Center, a community mental health center in a large midwestern city, completed an assessment on a client named Shannon and indicated that I might like to work with her. Shannon was a nineteen-year-old single female who had experienced more than a dozen hospitalizations in the past eighteen months for suicidal thoughts and actions. "She's borderline, and will need a lot of monitoring," my colleague said. She took me into the psychiatrist's office, where Shannon was having an initial medication evaluation, to introduce us.

I was annoyed that my colleague had described Shannon as borderline, and I wanted to "rescue" her from that diagnostic category, even though it did fit her. During the 1980s, that diagnosis had become very popular, almost faddish, among clinical workers of all disciplines. While legitimate, it was much overused and had become a negative label among practitioners. All diagnoses are reductionistic, but the diagnosis of borderline personality disorder, with its criteria of impulsiveness, lability, self-destructive tendencies, and acting out, seemed particularly stigmatizing. But something about this young woman's unusually large number of hospitalizations intrigued me enough to accept the assignment. This assignment was also appropriate because of my dual role at the agency as a therapist and as the aftercare coordinator who provided case management services to seriously mentally ill clients.

The First Six Months

Shannon and I met one week later for the first time in a private interview. She was one and a half years out of high school and looked her age, with long,

New Directions for Mental Health Services, no. 65, Spring 1995 © Jossey-Bass Publishers sandy-brown hair, big-boned features, casual dress, and an athletic air. Her affect, however, was strikingly grim. Throughout the interview she rarely looked me in the eye or spoke, but sat still in her chair except for a shaking leg, which betrayed her anxiety. I did not react much to this behavior. Many clients are anxious during the early sessions, as they are questioned about their personal lives by a stranger with unclear motives. My goal, as always, was to get to know the client, help her articulate her needs, gather some personal history, tell her about my style of working, and perhaps set a few preliminary goals for intervention. I was troubled by her personal history, most of which I learned from the referral information. All of her hospitalizations had been due to suicidal depression. There was no history of any intervention prior to her high school graduation, and no sustained outpatient intervention since then. She was receiving antidepressant medications from the agency psychiatrist.

I learned about her family circumstances during the next few weeks. Shannon was the fourth of eight children born to a Catholic couple, and the fourth girl. The family was middle-class but upwardly mobile. Her father was a successful salesman. Her parents had a rural background but moved to a suburban area when Shannon was five years old. Shannon recalled a childhood of neglect, remembering that her parents left all cooking, cleaning, laundering, and other household routines to the children. She later stated that she did not get along with any of her siblings and was frequently scapegoated and ridiculed. As a teenager, she took long walks through her neighborhood each night to escape the chaos and demeaning atmosphere of her homelife.

Shannon had been an average student but exhibited superior athletic ability. She captained several championship athletic teams at her high school. Still, she had no close girlfriends. On the day after her graduation, she moved into the home of an older male friend, his two adolescent children, and two other female acquaintances. She had become acquainted with them while working as an emergency medical technician at the local volunteer fire department. Shannon had developed an early interest in nursing and by age eighteen was handling herself skillfully on rescue squad runs. She and her housemates were quite active, working long hours at the fire department, attending parties, playing sports, and going on weekend trips. It was clear that Shannon did not like to be alone, and kept busy whether or not she was interested in the activity of the moment. She was at best cordial with her family but had little contact with her parents and siblings, returning home only at Christmas.

In our early interviews, Shannon was not articulate about her history, her present circumstances, her mood, or anything else. She seemed extremely uncomfortable and claimed not to remember basic personal information such as her daily routines in high school. Her anxiety level tended to accelerate as our fifty-minute sessions progressed. When I learned that her male friend had pressured her into keeping appointments at the agency, I doubted she would remain in treatment for long. I suspected that Shannon, like many clients, was fulfilling a personal obligation, and would drop out once she could convince her friend that the process was not helpful. Still, I tried not to promote a self-fulfilling prophecy. I was interested in her; fascinated that she kept such an extreme emotional distance from everyone she knew. During those first weeks, it became clear to me that Shannon was going to be difficult to engage in a relationship. I tried to convey my desire to help her. I also did much more talking than I was accustomed to, as she did so little. She gave minimal responses to my questions about her mood, sleeping patterns, activity patterns, and relationships. I explained why I was asking, that I was concerned about her safety and needed information to be able to help. She gave no indication that my words made an impression. She was not hostile but seemed rather disdainful of the process to which she was being subjected. I saw Shannon as a possible suicide because she was so isolated and depressed.

As a matter of tradition, I scheduled Shannon for weekly sessions. Eventually, I realized that this was a mistake. Both of us, I am afraid, seemed to count the minutes until the end of each meeting. I became as anxious with Shannon as she was with me and dreaded the long silences that characterized our sessions. I was not sure how much I should say, whether I should try to draw her out, or become confrontational about her apparent indifference. I simply did not know her well enough to intervene with confidence. I spent time before each session getting mentally "psyched up" to meet with her, as I knew the hour would be a drain on my energy. Our initial listing of treatment goals, developed rather mechanically, included alleviation of her depression with the use of medications and improvement of her coping skills to prevent the recurrence of suicidal ideation.

For six months, I attempted to implement this plan through regular counseling sessions, but there was no apparent progress. Shannon attended about two-thirds of her scheduled sessions, rarely spoke, reluctantly agreed to follow-up sessions, and left. Sometimes, in frustration, I ended sessions a few minutes early, but was reluctant to do this often as she might perceive it as my desiring to be rid of her. In fact, I was conscious of wanting to be rid of the discomfort she generated in me.

Shannon was also quiet in her monthly appointments with the agency psychiatrist. She never acknowledged that the antidepressants he prescribed were helping her but seemed to acquiesce to their prescription. Her physician was concerned about her overdose potential and tried to maintain her at moderate dosage levels. We were never certain that she took the medication.

I occasionally received phone calls from her male friend, Ken. He called to report that she was threatening suicide and was missing appointments intentionally. He also offered details of her personal history. While Shannon had given me permission to speak to Ken, I did not like doing so and stopped after a few months. She seemed to be using him as her spokesman, and I was reluctant to reinforce this pattern.

Shannon dropped out of treatment after six months, and I could see little progress in our relationship or treatment. She seemed aware that she had problems, but what was most striking was her lack of connection to others. She had not developed any trust in me, despite my sincere but awkward efforts to engage her in treatment. Following agency protocol, I wrote a letter and phoned to request her return, but she did not respond. I was not relieved that she had dropped out, as was sometimes true with other difficult clients. Despite how anxious she made me, I had seen her as a challenge.

Case Management: Phase One

Two months later, I received a call from a social worker at the regional state hospital. Shannon had been admitted following a serious overdose of medications. I was asked to visit her and help with the staff's assessment and discharge planning. When I arrived on the second day of her hospitalization, Shannon seemed surprised by my visit. However, her affect was brighter, and she was more verbal than she had been in our prior meetings. During the next two years, Shannon was admitted to area hospitals approximately ten times, and the pattern of her admission and discharge was consistent. Always admitted because of suicidal ideation, she felt immediate relief upon admission and then worked for a quick release, which always occurred within four days.

She was discharged, and we resumed weekly meetings at the agency. For the first time, I experienced a sense of collaboration and connection as Shannon began to express her concerns and goals, which included meeting new friends and deciding on career goals. We worked uncertainly on these goals, as Shannon expressed considerable doubt in her ability to meet them. Shannon was still quiet for most of our sessions, claiming that she did not know what to say or how she felt. Many times we talked about nothing that could be considered substantive to her problems. To relieve the silence, I often talked with her about sports, her emergency services work, television shows, her friends—anything, really, that seemed to pique her interest. I felt awkward about proceeding this way for weeks on end but found it difficult to engage her in any other sort of conversation.

During this period, I initiated many environmental interventions. I made formal arrangements for her to use the local emergency services facility and developed relationships with social workers at the area psychiatric hospitals that Shannon utilized. I helped arrange for a review of her entitlement status for Medicaid with the county Department of Human Services and linked her with a nearby clubhouse where she attended social and group therapy activities two half-days a week. I also referred her to an eight-week assertiveness training program at our clinic as a means of helping her learn to communicate more easily. She was superficially agreeable to these referrals but was at best ambivalent about the programs.

In spite of my efforts, Shannon did not actively engage with the staff or clients in these other programs. The staff from those programs complained to me about her indifference and looked to me for direction. I recommended that they tolerate Shannon's withdrawn behavior and offer her an opportunity to become engaged. Of course, I was not confident that this would happen.

Her hospitalizations during this time, numbering six during that first year, were precipitated by her depression, fear of losing self-control, and the alarming anxiety she experienced when alone. These episodes often occurred during her chronically sleepless nights, when she would lie in bed for hours and experience escalating terror about losing control of herself.

I continued to experience anxiety in our sessions because of the lengthy silences. I remained uncertain how much to push Shannon to be more responsive and how much conversation to initiate myself. This was unusual for me, as I generally feel confident in my ability to develop relationships with seriously disturbed clients. We were now meeting twice weekly on a more consistent basis. I had suggested this nine months after our first contact, as a means of improving object constancy in her relationship with me.

During this period, I sought consultation on my work with Shannon. However, the first time I presented Shannon's case in a staff meeting, the outcome was upsetting for me. Several respected staff members challenged me on key treatment issues. One suggested that I should not push Shannon at all, either to talk or to attend sessions. After all, it was her responsibility to invest in the process if anything positive was going to develop. This person added that the prognosis for change was poor because of the severity of Shannon's detachment. Next, the clinical director criticized me for allowing Shannon to become dependent on me. Instead of providing me with a fresh outlook and new strategies, this consultation made me feel more inadequate. Now I was anxious not only about the clinical relationship but also about the reactions of my colleagues. Although shaken, I disagreed with their observations. I saw Shannon as too fragmented to adhere to a treatment plan without support, and further, I needed to allow her to develop a dependence on me as a step toward developing trust. I saw Shannon as dealing with such inner turmoil that she simply could not yet risk opening up with anyone for fear of rejection.

This consultation did stimulate self-reflection on my countertransference responses. I was frequently drawn to the most difficult agency clients, due to what I perceived as an ability to empathize and connect with them. But sometimes I wondered if I might be masochistic or had a need to be needed that was prompting me to overly accommodate Shannon's resistant behaviors. Nevertheless, I decided to continue with my approach for a while longer. Despite my disappointment, I presented Shannon in our staff meetings about forty times during the seven years we worked together.

Two Years On: A Breakthrough

As our third year began, the relationship reached the most significant turning point of our work together. Shannon was again experiencing self-destructive thoughts and fears of losing control, and I facilitated her admission to a short-term crisis residence. She was there less than a week when I received a call from the program director. Shannon had written a lengthy narrative for me and had asked if I could come to pick it up. Further, she had asked to be driven to our agency for a session with me on the following day. I was extremely curious and hurried across town to the facility. Shannon asked that I wait until returning to the office to read her ten-page letter. In it, she detailed her history of sexual abuse by her father, which spanned the ages of five through seventeen. She recalled few details of the incidents but had consciously withheld this information from me. She had never discussed these incidents with anyone else. Shannon added that the incest was her own fault; proof that she was a disgusting human being. There was to be no salvation for her, and it meant that she could never become close to anyone.

When we met the next day, Shannon wept and shook throughout the hour. I wound up talking for most of the session once it became clear that she was not able to say much. I acknowledged reading the letter and expressed my horrified reaction to her revelations. I told her that I was not surprised by her story, as I had always suspected this possibility. I stated that I thought no less highly of her and restated my commitment to helping her heal these wounds and improve her life.

I asked Shannon how she had expected me to react to her letter. She feared that I would refuse to see her anymore because she was such a bad person. She then wondered how long it would be before she no longer needed counseling. I said I did not know and did not want to guess and perhaps be wrong. However, I would continue working with her indefinitely. I ended the session by arranging another meeting at the crisis center prior to her return home. I jokingly asked if the meeting had been as bad as she had expected. She smiled and shook her head. As she left the office, I restrained my impulse to hug her.

Several months later I asked Shannon why she had finally decided to tell me about the incest. She said little but later responded in a letter that she never trusted anyone and assumed that anyone who knew her secret would reject her. She also admitted to feeling confused by my persistent interest in her as I followed her from hospital to hospital and called her when she missed sessions. She wondered what I had wanted from her and suspected that my motives were ultimately sexual. Shannon also told me that she had experienced my service linkages as strategies to either get rid of or embarrass her in front of other service providers. She resented my referrals except as a means of possibly escaping my influence. It was only after our first year of work that she had considered that I might be interested in her welfare.

Case Management: Phase Two

During our third year, Shannon made a decision to commit herself to the treatment process. We continued to meet twice weekly in the office, focusing more directly now on our relationship in the context of her admission of incest, her coping with depression, her relationships with family and others, and her desire to eradicate her sense of emptiness. Shannon was more verbal now at times but still far less so than my other clients. We discussed our relationship and how effectively we were communicating with each other, as well as the topics related to her treatment goals.

Shannon openly asked for help with a number of concrete issues, and my environmental interventions increased. I now knew of her negative reactions to my earlier case management referrals, so now we worked more collaboratively in selecting other supports. Like many clients with borderline personality disorder, Shannon tended to fill her internal void with as much externally focused activity as possible. Now, She was eager to pursue activity everywhere. She sometimes scheduled her days with eighteen hours of commitments, working many day-long shifts at the fire department, traveling with her friends on weekend outings in which she was minimally interested, and taking continuing education courses at a junior college. Although I believed that her hyperactivity was a defense against her emerging feelings of anxiety and depression, I was reluctant to discourage her from taking initiatives to address her self-identified needs. Shannon asked for my help in establishing many program linkages, most of which involved volunteer activities. She eventually abandoned many of these commitments as she became overwhelmed.

As one example, Shannon learned of treatment groups being formed at a regional children's hospital for survivors of incest aged eight and younger. The groups utilized volunteers as co-leaders and included adult survivors in this role. Shannon asked for my help in applying for such a position. I agreed to do so as she felt she could maintain the commitment. As I feared, Shannon completed the training but had to resign after two weeks as a group co-leader. She became depressed and again was briefly hospitalized. I worried about my role in this failure. However, her brief group participation helped her see that no six-year-old child can be responsible for initiating or terminating such sexual behavior from an adult. Understanding the helplessness of the children, she began to feel less guilty about her victimization.

Shannon still needed more daily structure as a way to avoid periods of loneliness. Near the end of our fourth year, I referred her to another clubhouse program, which she attended three days weekly. Shannon participated marginally but remained a member for her full six-month term, evidence of an improved tolerance for social interaction. I attended staff meetings there at least once every two weeks to promote consistency in her care and help the staff understand her modest level of participation.

Shannon was working hard on her problems during our third and fourth years but often felt that she was losing control. Still, she was not hospitalized as often. In fact, each year she experienced 50 percent fewer hospitalizations. Her inpatient stays, however, became longer, largely at my instigation, since I saw them as opportunities to explore some of her more traumatic issues in a safe environment. During this period, she could now describe her negative feelings without precipitating unmanageable regression. When she experienced a crisis, she could work more collaboratively with me and other outpatient service providers to recompensate without hospitalization.

I was often frustrated by difficulties collaborating with staff from the hospitals and other programs, usually from disciplines other than social work. They often disagreed with my treatment approach and implemented new intervention strategies without consulting me. This was particularly problematic because Shannon was so remote and difficult to assess; she was a blank canvas onto which anyone could project a diagnostic image. I had many conflicts with ward psychiatrists who wanted to change her medication as the intervention of first resort, disrupting our agency's ongoing pharmacological strategy. Thus, I attempted to form alliances with hospital social workers who could advocate for my positions in their treatment team meetings.

In the fourth year of treatment, Shannon expressed a desire to work more directly on her incest issues. She had read several books about childhood sexual abuse that I recommended, and her memories of abuse incidents gradually emerged. I referred her to a group for incest survivors. She was not ready to discuss her secrets and soon dropped out.

Fortunately, Shannon gradually began to make small, but significant, changes that affirmed my treatment approach. During our fourth year, she had quit volunteering at the fire department and entered a program to become a licensed practical nurse. She still had few actual friends but was attending the clubhouse program regularly and spending time with her classmates. For a time, she worked with great success as a nurse's aide in a major hospital, although she complained that she was merely fooling people about her performance. Eventually, she took a job as a bus driver for persons with physical disabilities. The job had flexible hours and enabled her to attend the nursing program full time. She became the most reliable employee at the transit company and could even feel some pride in her exemplary performance. Even so, she was often depressed and often sought outpatient treatment at our community's emergency services.

Another major breakthrough occurred during the fifth year, when I again referred her to a therapy group at another agency for survivors of incest. We had been considering her reenrollment in such a group for several months. After researching available resources, I coordinated her entry into a group whose leader seemed willing to respect her defenses and avoid confrontation. In this weekly group, Shannon finally functioned as an active participant. Over a thirty-two-week period, she learned about incest from others who had been in the same situation and were at various stages in the recovery process. She connected with the other members, formed some lasting friendships, and began to display a brighter affect. Shannon and I often discussed her group experiences in our individual sessions, noting her increasing social skills.

As Shannon became more involved with others, I became concerned about her ongoing dependence, as she continued to rely on me to intervene with other professionals on her behalf. I wondered if my own need to be in control was getting in the way of our work. I raised this issue regularly with supervisors and colleagues—so often that I became concerned that I was dwelling on Shannon too much at the expense of other clients on my caseload. However, as her recovery and growth became more evident, I became less anxious about these issues.

When she was twenty-four, midway through our fifth year, Shannon proudly received her licensed practical nurse degree. She sent me a formal invitation to her graduation, accompanied by a personal letter that thanked me for my support over the years. I attended her graduation, although I rarely attend personal events in my clients' lives. I visited with her briefly after the ceremony but did not attend her reception.

The Final Eighteen Months

Six months after her graduation, Shannon abruptly announced plans to move to Colorado. She was experiencing a great deal of distress about her family and home environment since reviving memories of her abusive childhood. She had increased her social contact with several siblings but not her parents. On the one hand, her planned move seemed to express a desire for more autonomy and independence, and on the other hand, she seemed to want to flee from difficult intrapsychic and interpersonal issues. I did not enthusiastically support the plan because of her continued fragility, but neither did I strongly object, as the plan was an expression of her emerging autonomy. When she finally moved to Colorado to live with a friend, I arranged a referral to a local counseling center. Unfortunately, she relapsed within two months after her move and was hospitalized; the first of three lengthy inpatient episodes during the year she spent in that locale.

According to a six-month plan we devised before she moved, I called her monthly, and she also wrote letters. I wrote to her treatment providers to arrange for occasional phone consultations but received little cooperation in this regard. Most of the clinicians with whom I spoke utilized a more confrontational clinical approach. Medications and diagnoses were frequently changed. However, when her therapist in Colorado suggested she had both multiple personality and eating disorders and attempted to initiate hypnotherapy, Shannon returned to our community, disappointed by her attempted foray into independence.

When Shannon returned, she was immediately hospitalized and to my great surprise was administered a series of electroconvulsive treatments (ECT). I was angered at this decision by the hospital physician, as he did not consult with me or with our agency psychiatrist. Shannon did feel less depressed for several months afterward, but many of her memories of the past year were wiped out, making any review of her year away almost impossible. Also, I was unable to obtain her records from Colorado. When I finally made phone contact with her outpatient clinician there to request her records, I was lectured about how to organize my work with Shannon in order to maintain the momentum they had developed.

Although she resumed employment as a nurse, Shannon was again more quiet, withdrawn, and insecure. At the beginning of our seventh year of work, she again attempted suicide. During a hospitalization, Shannon was unexpectedly visited on three occasions by her parents, whom she had not seen in four years except at extended family gatherings. As Shannon preferred not to see them, I advised the hospital staff to prohibit family visits after the first meeting. However, when her parents returned, she was unable to tell her father she did not want to see him. The reason for these visits was never clear, but they followed Shannon's sending her father a letter explaining that she now understood that the incest was his fault. Shannon and I had also been discussing her desire to confront him in person about the abuse. I warned her that he might never acknowledge responsibility for his behavior and that it would be some time before she was ready for a confrontation of that magnitude.

After the third visit, Shannon left the hospital on a grounds pass, walked across the street to a parking garage, and leapt from the fourth-story wall. Miraculously, she survived. In fact, she was barely injured, as her fall was broken by trees. An employee who had witnessed the jump called an ambulance, but the next day she was transferred back to the psychiatric facility. This was her first actual suicide attempt in five years and also her last, but it was quite serious. I was angry at the hospital staff for not enforcing my prescribed limit, at her parents for intruding on our work, and at Shannon for still lacking the ability to assert herself.

This incident reminded me again of Shannon's vulnerability to severe depression. When stressed, in this case by her father's evoking strong feelings of her loathsome self, she could lose sight of her gains and assume that she was not changing. At these times I recounted her gains, but Shannon responded that she doubted treatment was helping her anymore. Privately, I wondered whether her core of emptiness would ever fill to a point where she would not need intervention.

Termination

By the middle of the sixth year, we had reduced the frequency of our sessions from twice to once weekly. This had been done to accommodate Shannon's work schedule at a convalescent center, but it was also in response to her increased external supports, including several new friends. A few months later, Shannon enrolled in a registered nursing program in a city fifty miles away and moved there while keeping a part-time weekend job in our community. She successfully avoided her parents, even while serving as a bridesmaid in her sister's wedding. She shared an apartment now with a friend from her incest survivors group and participated with a new group of acquaintances from school and her work site. Change was also evident in Shannon's affect. She became able to express feelings about me, most frequently in her occasional letters but also by asking for hugs (which I did share with her) after difficult sessions. At times, she even expressed anger at me, criticizing me for not being more directive about how she should structure her days.

When she left town to enroll in nursing school, Shannon began a process of termination that I ignored for several months. She continued commuting to our weekly sessions when she came to town for her weekend work. She was appropriately focused on her current school and work issues and was less interested in discussing her traumatic childhood. She had reconciled herself to the idea that she would not be a participant in her parents' lives any longer and defended against her painful memories by minimizing her contact with them.

After seven years of our working together, Shannon failed an appointment and did not respond to my subsequent messages about rescheduling. When several weeks elapsed with no word from her, I became concerned, as this was unusual. One month later, I received a letter from her that politely informed me that she had decided to end our relationship and pursue her life in a new location without therapy or medication. She wrote that she would have told me in person except that I always talked her out of termination when she brought it up. This time she felt sure of herself and did not want to expose her decision to my therapeutic scrutiny. I had mixed feelings about this decision, as I did about almost everything in her case. But I immediately wrote back to support her decision, affirming her steady progress and inviting her to return in the future if she felt the need. I did not express my ambivalence, because I felt that this was an important move on her part toward independence.

Eight months later, I accepted a job out of state and wrote Shannon to notify her of my leaving. She wrote back, as I hoped she would. She thanked me for my help over the years, wished me well, and updated me on her life. I was pleased to learn that she was progressing in her work on the nursing degree, had a good job in the nursing field, was living with a new female friend, had a boyfriend, and was not in counseling or taking medication. It was a rewarding goodbye from her.

Discussion

There are three themes that I feel are important to highlight concerning my work with Shannon. These include the importance of case management for a nonpsychotic client, the element of timing in linkage activities, and the countertransference that Shannon evoked in me and other service providers.

Many clients in the public mental health system have serious mental illnesses but are not generally psychotic. They have complex personality disorders that demand careful therapeutic management rather than psychosocial rehabilitation or clinically pristine psychotherapy. Diagnostic labels in any case are of limited utility in treatment planning. Shannon's case represents a persuasive argument for the case manager's performing both psychodynamic and environmental interventions (Harris and Bergman, 1993; Kanter, 1989). Had I not been intimately involved in decisions about referral agencies and maintained contact with her during hospitalizations, she would not have engaged in treatment or would have terminated prematurely. Shannon, who usually said so little, emphasized that it was my persistence in following her to hospitals and other agencies that eventually, after almost two years, convinced her that I could be trusted as a helper. Had I limited my availability to more conventional office or even telephone contacts, she might never have returned after that initial hospitalization.

In the late 1980s, the policy of our state department of mental health was changing and would not tolerate the "clinical case manager" modality any longer. By 1989, our county mental health planning board took the position that case managers should only perform environmental interventions and opposed the concept of the clinical case manager who performs both tasks. What had once been a smoothly functioning generalist agency milieu became programmatically factionalized. The case management program was subsequently staffed with lesser educated and experienced workers without clinical training. Case managers were expected to link clients to services and offer a sort of generic support. In this model, a case manager would have tried to socialize Shannon, who was classified as having a serious mental illness, exclusively into programs for that client population and might have overlooked her strengths for returning to normal community functioning (Kanter, 1989). This would have been inadequate, because Shannon's life-threatening psychiatric disorder required a recognition of the sequelae of a history of childhood sexual abuse (Redner and Herder, 1992), including knowing when to explore and when to respect defenses, tolerating transference and countertransference reactions, collaborating with professional providers in hospitals, and understanding that her living skills were much greater than her skills for coping with illness. Additionally, my clinical case management with Shannon can also be characterized by what I did not do with her. I did not rush to engage her in support and rehabilitation programs or enlist her in the "patient" role. I spent much time getting to know her and learning about her strengths for independent living. I raise this issue as an illustration of how policies can hamper the provision of good clinical care when they are implemented without concern for individual client circumstances. Much good has resulted from the county's new case management programs, but the needs of many clients like Shannon have been neglected.

During my first two years of case management with Shannon, most of my efforts to link her with other programs were failures. I followed a sort of conventional case management protocol in suggesting service activities for her, but some were ill timed. Further, she told me that she interpreted my efforts to link her with other services as attempts to abandon her but never expressed this until later in our relationship. She struggled with an approach-avoidance dilemma (McMillen, 1992), and it was only my persistence and refusal to place demands on her that helped Shannon eventually work through her ambivalence. It took two years before I developed enough understanding of Shannon to intervene empathically with her environment and before she would trust me to do this without making matters worse. This is not unusual for clients with serious mental illness, but because Shannon was quiet and superficially agreeable, I overestimated her readiness for those initial linkage activities.

Finally, Shannon demonstrates the intense countertransference that a suicidal client with a severe personality disorder can evoke in providers (Kanter, 1988). She elicited a helplessness that I and others defended against with various rescue techniques (that is, medications, ECT, hypnosis, linkage activities).

She repeatedly created situations where I found myself competing with other professionals, particularly in times of crisis when my work was open to criticism. This made my case management activities difficult. While I attempted to coordinate care between hospitals, emergency service facilities, and other agencies, the long-term treatment plan I had devised with the agency psychiatrist was disrupted by other professionals who responded only to the immediate crisis. My sense of inadequacy was exacerbated by the status differential between my position and that of the hospital staff. Developing collaborative relationships with these people, especially social workers, was essential for maintaining continuity of care. I imagine that case managers without professional training and the program coordinator status that I held would have even more problems maintaining continuity of care with this type of client.

When working with persons with serious mental illness, my desire to help them achieve full recovery often conflicts with my intellectual knowledge that such outcomes are often not possible. Nonetheless, I often ignore my less-optimistic colleagues and strive for more ambitious goals. My early intervention strategy with Shannon was based on a desire to prevent her dropping out of treatment. On reflection, I feel that what effectiveness I eventually had was based on a recognition that Shannon had considerable strength in spite of her repeated hospitalizations and her inability to develop a healthy dependence on others. Further, my encouragement of her to seek support from others besides myself helped obviate her fears of incestuous merger. My environmental interventions represented a way of publicly relating to her, as I did not restrict our interactions to more threatening private meetings.

As our relationship developed, I became acutely aware that I was the only person she trusted. This frightened me in some ways, as it made me feel rather responsible for her welfare. I was also concerned about her ability to work with a man, particularly when her incest history emerged. But when I explored this with her on various occasions she actually stated a preference for men, although never articulating her reasons. As our relationship progressed, I referred her to programs and therapy groups where she could become more comfortable relating to women as well. However, over the long run, our relationship may have taught Shannon that she can care for and be cared for by a man without sexual abuse or emotional exploitation. Such reparative experiences may be more valuable than analytic interpretations (Markowitz, 1992).

One thing I would do differently if I were working with Shannon again is seek individual supervision. This would allow me to focus more specifically on countertransference issues than intervention techniques. Because of their unfamiliarity with the therapeutic case management modality, experienced agency clinicians often exacerbated my insecurity instead of offering support. In turn, the case managers I consulted with tended to focus rather simplistically on available community resources and systems issues.

There are two other issues I struggled with over the years. First, I wondered if Shannon's growth might have been achieved sooner; if I should have had higher expectations for her taking responsibility for her own well-being.

She had been a suicide risk, primarily during the first few years, and my initial referrals for supplemental care had not been successful. I allowed her to move slowly during the next five years, sometimes feeling impatient with her, and was not firm about her following through with certain difficult activities including participation in other programs. However, I now understand that greater firmness might have been viewed by Shannon as a kind of rape, an intrusion on her developing autonomy. Second, I felt at times that I should have done more legwork in the linkage process. That is, I should have spent more time at area hospitals, clubhouses, and emergency service facilities prior to my need for their services in an effort to establish credibility and clarify my expectations for their work with Shannon. But again, this was unrealistic. One cannot avoid the phenomenon of splitting with persons having borderline personality disorder (Masterson, 1981).

In summary, I learned much from Shannon about the coping strategies of survivors of sexual abuse. While we never had a formal termination session, I have imagined how she might have summarized her reasons for leaving treatment: "I'm tired of dwelling on my past. I don't want to keep talking and thinking about the incest with my dad. I've learned how to get on with my life and keep the bad experiences in a certain part of my mind. They don't intrude on my awareness all the time. I can work, have friends, take care of myself, live independently, and work toward my personal goals. That's all I want. That's what most people have." I once thought that an incest survivor needed to thoroughly resolve her abuse issues, to confront and work through them all. Shannon taught me that I was wrong, that people have different strengths and coping styles and come to terms with trauma differently. Shannon has indeed gotten on with her life.

References

Harris, M., and Bergman, H. C. (eds.). *Case Management for Mentally Ill Patients: Theory and Practice.* Langhorne, Pa.: Harwood, 1993.

Kanter, J. S. "Clinical Issues in the Case Management Relationship." In M. Harris and L. Bachrach (eds.), *Clinical Case Management.* New Directions for Mental Health Services, no. 40. San Francisco: Jossey-Bass, 1988.

Kanter, J. S. "Clinical Case Management: Definition, Principles, Components." *Hospital and Community Psychiatry,* 1989, *40,* 361–368.

McMillen, J. C. "Attachment Theory and Clinical Social Work." *Clinical Social Work Journal,* 1992, *20,* 205–218.

Markowitz, L. M. "Reclaiming the Light." *Family Therapy Networker,* 1992, *16* (3), 17–27.

Masterson, J. F. *The Narcissistic and Borderline Disorders: An Integrated Developmental Approach.* New York: Brunner/Mazel, 1981.

Redner, L. I., and Herder, D. D. "Case Management's Role in Effecting Appropriate Treatment for Persons with Histories of Childhood Sexual Trauma." *Psychosocial Rehabilitation Journal,* 1992, *15* (3), 37–45.

JOSEPH WALSH, Ph.D., L.C.S.W., is assistant professor in the School of Social Work, Virginia Commonwealth University, Richmond, Virginia.

Commentary

Maxine Harris, Ph.D.
Co-director, Community Connections
Washington, D.C.

Joseph Walsh is to be commended for his caring and sensitive work with Shannon. Without his consistent involvement in her life, she would have been a casualty of her traumatic abuse history. In the ten years since he began his work with her, many advances have been made in the treatment of trauma survivors that add insight to the case presented here. These advances include the role of assessment, the importance of accurate diagnosis, the role of case management, the role of support groups, the use of male clinicians, the pattern of institutional revictimization, the nature of recovery, and the necessity for support and supervision of clinicians who work with trauma survivors.

Despite her many contacts with mental health practitioners, Shannon seems never to have been asked directly about her abuse history. Because of her guardedness, Shannon might have been unlikely to answer a direct question honestly. However, many women with similar histories do respond honestly to routine assessment questions about sexual and physical abuse (Rose, Peabody, and Stratigeas, 1991). By including questions about abuse as part of standard intake, clinicians make abuse an acceptable part of the clinical dialogue rather than keeping it as a secret that can not be discussed.

Accurate assessment leads to accurate diagnosis. Walsh foreshadowed our shifting diagnostic perspective when he expressed his uneasiness with the label borderline. Many trauma survivors have expressed their own displeasure with this diagnosis, suggesting that it is not only inaccurate but unduly stigmatizing. Researchers such as Judith Herman have offered "complex post traumatic disorder" as a more accurate diagnosis for trauma survivors (Herman, 1992).

Walsh is correct in suggesting a clinical case management intervention with Shannon. However, this modality must be modified and tailored for work with trauma survivors (Harris, 1994). Case management with trauma survivors must be genuinely and explicitly collaborative. No intervention should be undertaken without the client's consent. The rationale for every referral should be clearly stated. Clients must always have the right to say "no" to a referral. Given their abuse histories, clients are legitimately wary of any suggestion made "for their own good" by an authority figure.

After two problematic attempts, Shannon eventually made a successful connection to a trauma recovery group. In addition to benefiting from individual work, most trauma survivors benefit from participation in a support and psychoeducational group. In a group, survivors gain needed information about trauma and are able to challenge their mistaken assumptions about causality and personal responsibility. They also hear the stories of other survivors and come to place their personal histories in a shared context. Just as Shannon did, many survivors meet other survivors via the group who become an important part of their support network.

As their work progressed, Shannon revealed to Walsh her early belief that he, like all men, was only interested in sex. This is the dilemma faced by male clinicians who treat female trauma survivors. The survivor has no reason to believe that this male clinician will be any different than past male abusers. In those cases where cross-gender therapy succeeds, Walsh is correct that the client learns a valuable lesson: not all men are abusers. However, in most cases the clinician makes a careless slip that marks him as an abuser in the client's mind, rendering him ineffective as a caregiver, or the client terminates therapy early in the process.

While I believe that female clinicians are, in general, better suited to work with female trauma survivors, they are not themselves free of transference distortions from the client's history of abuse. While most abusers of women were men, most trauma survivors had a naïve, absent, or impotent mother who was witness to the abuse. Consequently, trauma survivors may treat female clinicians with contempt, anger, or hopelessness. Regardless of gender, clinicians should anticipate mistaken expectations that might interfere with the work. They should discuss these openly both early and often in the treatment.

Because Walsh was a consistent advocate, Shannon suffered few of the institutional abuses reported by trauma survivors. However, even with his involvement, she still had to endure a series of shock treatments. More often than not, trauma survivors report being retraumatized by the treatment system that is intended to help them. Aggressive and intrusive interventions such as involuntary hospitalization, over- or forced medication, use of seclusion, and use of physical restraints all make the trauma survivor feel out of control, powerless, and victimized. What is designed to be treatment may in fact leave the trauma survivor feeling vulnerable and helpless—the very feelings generated by the original abuse.

It is significant that Shannon made the decision to terminate her therapy on her own. She suspected, probably correctly, that her therapist would try to convince her to reconsider her plan to terminate. An important step in the recovery of any trauma survivor occurs when the survivor trusts her own judgment over the judgment of a trusted authority. The secrecy and deception that surround sexual abuse assault a child's faith in her view of the world. As a woman recovers from the psychological damage caused by abuse, she must gradually relearn to trust her own perception of things. Paradoxically, the good work Shannon did with Walsh allowed her to feel secure enough to terminate without his approval or his consent.

Walsh correctly concludes his paper with a recognition of the importance of supervision for the clinician attempting trauma work. Peer or group supervision provides the clinician with much-needed feedback and validation. Equally important is that the clinical setting in which the work occurs needs to be supportive. Clinicians must feel that they have a mandate from their supervisors and the backing of administrators when they embark on high-risk work. The work of trauma recovery is difficult and stressful for both client and clinician; clinic administrators have a responsibility to ensure that recovery work is not traumatizing for clinicians.

Commentary References

Harris, M., "Modifications in Service Delivery and Clinical Treatment for Women Diagnosed with Severe Mental Illness Who Are Also the Survivors of Sexual Abuse Trauma." *Journal of Mental Health Administration*, 1994, *21*, 397–406.

Herman, J. L., *Trauma and Recovery*. New York: Basic Books, 1992.

Rose, S. M., Peabody, C. G., and Stratigeas, B. "Undetected Abuse Among Intensive Case Management Clients." *Hospital and Community Psychiatry*, 1991, *42*, 499–502.

Covering a twenty-year period, this case report describes how community and hospital professionals collaborated to stop the "revolving door" and facilitate the recovery of a woman with a borderline personality disorder.

Passing the Baton: Four Perspectives on a Long-Term Treatment

Barbara Zimmann Caceres, Joel Kanter, Jack Barber, Carolyn Maurer
Commentary by Robert W. Surber

In this case report, four clinicians share their experience over the past thirteen years of working with Sharon, a thirty-five-year-old white woman with a history of childhood sexual abuse, over twenty-five psychiatric hospitalizations by age twenty-five, and a chart full of psychiatric diagnoses, most notably borderline personality disorder and schizoaffective disorder. She was treated in the same mental health system for over twenty years. This presentation encompasses both community and hospital interventions with three clinicians—Carolyn Maurer, Joel Kanter, and Barbara Caceres—describing their work at the Mount Vernon Center for Community Mental Health, and Jack Barber describing a lengthy hospital stay at Western State Hospital, which was a turning point for this very troubled woman. This complex case report is presented by the current case manager (Caceres) and interspersed with first-person narratives by the other three clinicians (Maurer first, then Barber, then Kanter). The concluding discussion is presented jointly.

Case Report

Sharon was an only child born to working-class parents, and her early childhood was marked by intense parental discord. Her father physically abused both her mother and herself. She recalls one instance when her father hacked through the door with an ax while she and her mother (who had locked him out of the house) hid in a locked bedroom. When Sharon was fifteen, her mother was hospitalized for a hysterectomy, and during her absence, Sharon's father fondled and raped her, stating that "you're going to do for me what your mother won't." When she told her mother about the incident, her mother replied that she was not going to ruin her life for Sharon and did nothing about it.

Angry at the lack of maternal support, Sharon took an overdose of aspirin, cut herself, and presented for intake at the mental health center complaining of depression. Treated in individual, group, and family therapies, she was able to graduate from high school, get a job, and live in an apartment with a friend. She eventually got married. But her suicidal gestures, mood instability, and regular slashing of arms and legs to "relieve tension" caused increasingly significant disruptions in her functioning, and put her at high risk in the community. Carolyn Maurer, the therapist and case manager who worked with Sharon from ages twenty-one to twenty-seven, describes the first stages of her treatment.

> It was emotionally draining because she was in continuous crisis, with as many as five hospitalizations a year. When we met, we would deal with her separation anxiety, loss issues, expression of anger, dependency, social isolation, and self-destructive behavior. Often she would refuse to talk in scheduled sessions then call later to say she was suicidal. It was scary always seeming to be dancing on the brink with her. I knew that if things were getting better or going well they would eventually crash, and if they were crashing, it seemed that any intervention was doomed to fail. When she started to spiral downhill, there was almost always a steady progression of her upping the ante; yet sometimes she would start to climb out of the spiral, so it kept people invested in trying to help her— and burned them out. Despite placing her in increasingly structured holding environments in the community, every intervention seemed doomed. Nothing we did was enough.
>
> If possible, we tried to keep her out of the hospital. Like most people with severe borderline personality disorder, she would regress dramatically once she was admitted, and the hospital would have difficulty discharging her. Sharon was highly sensitive to her parents' judgments about being sick and being an inpatient and had internalized the expectation that "if I go in the hospital one more time they'll disown me." Even when she knew she needed to be in the hospital, she could not go in voluntarily because she was so sure of her parents' disapproval. She would fight admission tooth and nail, and we would always have to detain her involuntarily. Yet there was always this enormous pull to go back to the hospital, as if her life script read: "I can't make it outside the hospital."
>
> Contact with Sharon's parents fluctuated depending on her willingness to have them involved. Her mother would join sessions from time to time to express concerns about Sharon, and while she tried to be supportive, she always seemed to have difficulty comprehending whether Sharon's behavior was sick or willful. Her own emotional deprivation was so great she had difficulty handling Sharon's neediness, felt overwhelmed by it, and often responded in a sadistic or punitive fashion. Sharon had become a management nightmare. Crisis intervention and collaboration with other staff around her emergencies and sui-

cidality took enormous amounts of time, and we felt increasingly frustrated and helpless. She burned out programs as well as individual staff members, causing all sorts of systems barriers to further referrals. Essentially, she was behaving as an inpatient in an outpatient setting, so we told her that if she wanted to be treated as an outpatient (which was her stated goal) then she would have to start acting like one. We stopped doing over-the-phone assessments of suicidality: if she called and was suicidal, we insisted she come to the center for assessment. When she presented with a carved tic-tac-toe design on her stomach and was assessed to be not suicidal, I sent her to the hospital to get checked out medically for tetanus. This was an attempt to disengage her from the emotional game-playing that always seemed to be going on.

Although these strategies helped, it eventually became clear that outpatient treatment was inadequate. She clearly needed the structure and boundaries of a long-term hospital setting that could offer her the opportunity to regress and recompensate over an extended period. She eventually got this opportunity for long-term treatment at Western State Hospital. I feel the mental health system collectively made a valiant effort to maintain her in the community. Our many efforts may not have made a big difference with her at that time, but they did help us learn to work with subsequent clients who have challenged us in similar ways.

The Western State Hospital admission—Sharon's sixth (at age twenty-seven)—was initially intended to stabilize an acute episode, but she remained in a persistent regression with interpersonal discord and significant acting-out, including cutting, head banging, suicidal gestures, destruction of property, and attacks on her attending physician. After six months on an admitting unit, she was transferred to the chronic unit, where she remained for the rest of her almost two-year stay. Jack Barber, Sharon's unit psychiatrist, describes her time on his unit.

Staff let out a collective groan when Sharon returned to our unit. Within the first week she assaulted another patient. Why us? What were we going to do with her? How were we going to manage her? She was regularly banging her head, abrading her arms with erasers, and making superficial scratches on her wrists. She eloped from the unit on one occasion. She wrote long letters to her attending physician describing identity diffusion, a sense of inner badness, and fears of destructive action toward herself and others. During the first six months, she oscillated between periods of relatively high functioning (during which she was friendly and able to discuss issues with staff and attempted to become an auxiliary staff member on the ward), and periods in which she felt she was all alone in an inner battle between her "good" and "bad" self (during which she insisted on entangling staff in numerous discussions of whether they cared about her or wanted to help her).

Several interventions were made shortly after she came to the unit. First, we simplified her medication regimen and resisted all attempts by Sharon to increase the dose. I interpreted her intermittent complaints of auditory hallucinations as a simple reflection of the stress she was under. When she asked for more meds, I told her that while these might be an effective response to acute hallucinations, the long-term answer was to sort out what the particular stressors were and figure out a way to cope with them.

Second, staff took particular care to avoid placing any expectations on her. We basically told her that there was no guarantee that she would improve to the point of being able to leave the hospital but that we were hopeful and would continue to work with her toward that end. I told her that neither she nor I had the answers to her problems and that any solution would not come quickly; also, that it was likely her self-injurious behavior would continue, and we should have no expectation that it would stop.

Psychotherapy sessions were designed to provide support and to counteract the hopelessness and despair of her depressed periods and to provide reality testing when she was feeling good and thought she would never experience any difficulties again. She was told that the first step toward moving forward would be for her to develop the ability to "hold on" during periods when she was depressed and despairing, as she and I both knew from experience that these periods would end. We used the locked side of the ward as a holding environment for limited periods around episodes of self-injury or violence and set this holding period at forty-eight hours. The therapy sessions were set up very rigidly on a weekly, half-hour basis. No changes in her treatment regimen were considered except within the context of the session and consequent treatment-planning meetings. We gave her the message that if she wished to proceed to a point where she could leave the hospital, it was fine with us. We would continue to try to help her do so but we had no particular expectation of her in this regard. However, if she wished to stay in the hospital, that would be okay with us also.

The basic plan was to reduce Sharon's sense of urgency and her oscillation between attempting to be an auxiliary staff member and regressing to very infantile and self-injurious behavior. We took the focus off her problematic behavior and related to her more as a person who was to be respected and whose problems were legitimate and to be respected. Our job was to provide a holding environment and some resistance to her periodic flights into health and feelings of false well-being.

Her last self-injurious episode—cutting her wrists, throwing a chair through the window of the nurses' station on the locked unit, and banging her head—occurred eight months after admission to the unit, although she still had numerous periods when she became quite depressed and despairing and struggled with wanting to hurt herself and attempting not to. However, over the next six months, this struggle seemed to attenuate and the regression seemed less pronounced. While clearly very tenuous, she began relating with a greater degree of balance and maturity in her interpersonal style. She began a series of week-long passes home, which were generally quite positive from her perspective.

Sharon's initial demands to leave the hospital were typically based on a very superficial realization of the potential problems. Staff confronted her on this, and she became more attentive and reasonable in discussing the risks of leaving the hospital and potential management strategies for those problems. Since it appeared that she was not making further progress in an inpatient setting, we determined that she should take several passes home and evaluate whether in fact she wanted to continue in the hospital or to be discharged. We discussed the risks of her returning home, where she had experienced so much difficulty in the past, versus waiting in the hospital for a group home placement in the community. Given her relative emotional stability and more mature style of interacting with others, we felt it was reasonable for her to return to the community.

We held a number of discussions with her about what to do when she felt depressed and despairing or suicidal. These discussions were carefully worded in order to reduce the expectation that once she left the hospital she would manage without stress or setbacks, and we clearly confronted her sense that we expected her to do well once she left the hospital. We simply noted with her that life in the community would be difficult and that it was far from clear that she would not need to be rehospitalized. We noted that if she could get involved in a day program and form an alliance with her outpatient therapist she might be able to sustain herself well enough to avoid prolonged hospitalization in the future. I indicated that I thought it was highly likely that her symptoms would recur and that she would probably need to be rehospitalized at some point, but agreed that neither she nor I had any way of knowing for sure. During the final pass prior to discharge, Sharon was able to manage reasonably well and was discharged.

In a thorough and unusually helpful nine-page discharge summary, Barber recommended a residential placement, a structured day program and weekend activities, and no changes in medications for at least six months. He warned that Sharon would have difficulty engaging in the therapeutic process and urged outpatient staff to dampen her urgent demands to move ahead, and to minimize external expectations and repeatedly stress the need for her to be patient.

Maurer and Barber gave considerable attention to the assignment of an outpatient therapist when Sharon returned to the community. As community liaison to the state hospitals, Maurer had visited Sharon monthly in Western State and had monitored her improvement. In meetings with Barber and the hospital social worker, she discussed her burnout in working with Sharon, as well as Sharon's intense maternal transference toward her. Additionally, they all observed that Sharon responded well to Barber's firmness and hypothesized that a male therapist who could effectively maintain boundaries might prove helpful. The team discussed these concerns in depth with Sharon and included her as much as possible in their deliberations before selecting someone for her to work with. Joel Kanter, her case manager for the next seven years, takes up the story.

I had never met Sharon, but I knew of her reputation and her nine-inch stack of records. The thought of working with her inspired a mixture of anticipation and dread. Her reported stabilization at the hospital seemed credible, yet there was no certainty how long it would last when she actually returned to the community. My initial meeting with Sharon was pleasantly unremarkable, and we calmly reviewed her hospital experience and her doctor's recommendations for community treatment—essentially recommendations that Sharon make no dramatic life changes, including housing and employment, for the next year. Unlike most hospital discharge summaries, this write-up demonstrated great sensitivity, understanding, and practicality.

Given her background of childhood sexual abuse, we had considerable concern about her residence with her parents. I repeatedly asked how things were going at home. Sharon, now in her late twenties, expressed no anxiety about further abuse from her father and, surprisingly, seemed to enjoy his company somewhat more than her mother's. She was attending our community's psychosocial rehabilitation program where she functioned as a sort of assistant to the office manager. She had several friends in this program but tended to avoid participation in the group activities.

In our weekly meetings, we casually discussed her daily activities and social relationships. Sharon missed almost a third of these meetings, but I avoided any confrontation of this as I believed it was important for her to feel in control of her participation in our relationship. When she would express feelings of emptiness and frustration with her lack of direction, we would discuss her goals and hopes for the future but always in a relaxed way that placed no expectations on her to make changes.

In the first year of our relationship, Sharon frequently expressed her ambivalence regarding working with me. She expressed this to me directly, to Maurer (the unit supervisor and Sharon's former case manager), and to her psychiatrist. She attentively catalogued my deficiencies in order to establish an objective basis for her transfer request. While in many situations, we would quickly accede to such a request, the team decided to resist her efforts for several reasons. First, Barber had noted that she often made similar requests in the hospital and had predicted that she would make such a request soon after arriving in the community. He had recommended against making any changes in her treatment plan for the first year in response to any of her expected demands. We feared that changing case managers would soon lead to requests for changes in medication, day support, and other aspects of her community plan. Second, although she often complained about me, Sharon seemed to be engaged in meaningful conversations with me. Third, we had no eager volunteers on the staff to assume responsibility for working with Sharon, and we believed that my experience relative to other team members would enable me to cope more effectively with the sort of challenges she presented.

In one of our discussions about changing case managers, I read Sharon Barber's discharge prediction that she would wish to have a new worker. Overall, she seemed to accept our explanation that we were trying to maintain a successful treatment plan that focused on maintaining consistency and stability.

About eight months after her return to the community, Sharon was contacted by the coordinator of our young adult group home. They had a vacancy, and her application (submitted while she was in the hospital) was at the top of their waiting list. Unfortunately, they contacted Sharon and scheduled an appointment with her without asking me or her psychiatrist about her current status or treatment plan. Predictably, she was very enthusiastic about this possibility, and again I was placed in the position of resisting her stated wishes. She was quite angry at me about this and complained that I wanted to prevent her from becoming independent. I stated that I thought she would have a greater opportunity to be successful in this program if she did not pursue this placement until some time in the future. Other staff also disagreed with my position, accusing me of wanting to impose my wishes on Sharon and force her to remain in a home with the incest perpetrator. However, she again acceded to my wishes without much protest, suggesting that she needed someone to restrain her desire to plunge ahead into precocious independence. Having witnessed this pattern over her years as Sharon's case manager, Maurer supported this approach.

Almost on the anniversary of her return to the community, Sharon obtained, through her own efforts, a half-time job as a store clerk. As a Social Security Disability Income (SSDI) recipient, she was able to retain all her earnings without jeopardizing her disability pension or Medicare. In our second year of work, she often talked to me about applying for our supervised apartment program, and I responded very passively to these wishes, neither encouraging or discouraging her. At a clinic case conference held about a year after discharge, Barber joined us and indicated that we would know she was ready to move into a residential program when she became insistent on making such a move. He recommended that we gently resist her movement toward independence and allow her to push through it. When strains developed in her relationships with her parents, she requested that I help her to gain admittance to the clinic's apartment program. I gave her an application and told her that when she was ready she could fill it out. She returned the completed application to me six months later.

During this second year of work, Sharon became more comfortable with her positive feelings about me, recognizing that a firm treatment approach was bearing fruit and helping her avoid any rehospitalizations. On one occasion, she came into the office stating that she hated me, then quickly said, "How can I hate you when I care about you so much?"

About two years after her hospital discharge, she became increasingly distressed with her family relationships (especially with her mother) and entered our Crisis Care Home. She recompensated in this facility but firmly stated that she did not want to return to her parents' home. Responding to her insistence, I changed my position and became an advocate, along with the Crisis Care Home staff, for her admission to the Therapeutic Apartment Program. After two months in the crisis care facility, she was directly admitted to the apartment program and began working with Caceres, the residential counselor, twice weekly.

I reduced my frequency of meetings with Sharon from weekly to biweekly over the next year. During this time, Caceres and I frequently discussed Sharon's history and progress, and it gradually became evident that Sharon was developing a strong attachment. Clearly, Sharon found it easier to converse with a female case manager about critical sexual issues.

After about a year in the apartment program, Sharon received a Section 8 certificate, which she had applied for before her last hospital admission, enabling her to obtain her own apartment. Although she was excited about this opportunity, Caceres and I were dismayed as we both believed Sharon would find it difficult to live alone. While she had considerable conflict with her roommates, these tensions emerged most often when she felt neglected, and we believed her loneliness would increase when she lived on her own.

However, as these certificates were hard to obtain, we could understand that Sharon would not want to miss this opportunity. Although I explicitly warned her about the likelihood that she would become quite lonely at times in her own apartment, I took a neutral stance toward the move, viewing it as an experiment she could always learn from. Sharon experienced the neutral attitude as discouraging, but I wanted her to be prepared for the stress of living alone.

Fortunately, the apartment program at that time allowed clients to continue working with residential counselors while living in their own independent apartments; thus Sharon was able to continue working with Caceres. By this time, it was apparent that she had replaced me as the primary therapist and case manager in Sharon's mind, and over time, my and Sharon's appointments were scheduled on an as-needed basis. However, as I had earlier given Sharon the number of a business line that forwards to my home, she called me (and still does) every week or two during the evenings or weekends for support or crisis intervention, when other supports are unavailable.

When Joel Kanter approached me (Barbara Caceres) about working with Sharon in our apartment program, he emphasized her current situation and her year of stability following a lengthy stay in the state hospital. I was not aware of her reputation, so I entered the relationship with few preconceived notions. Here she had an opportunity to start fresh. We placed her in an apartment with two other women, and for the next two years, I met with her weekly at the office in addition to a group meeting at the apartment. In these settings she discussed a range of issues: her many chronic and incurable medical problems, her difficulties at work, her conflicts with roommates, her parents' neglect of her emotional needs, her mood swings, and her need to develop coping skills to deal with the stresses of daily living. Themes of dependency, loneliness, anxiety, and attachment were prominent throughout our work together.

Crises arose almost daily around her myriad chronic medical problems: asthma and cardiopulmonary disease that required frequent trips to the emergency room for breathing treatments and often inpatient hospitalizations; chronic back pain; arthritis; seizure disorder; thyroid nodules that required regular biopsies; recurring bronchitis, sinus infections, and pneumonia; high blood pressure; stomach problems. She spent much of her time in endless complaints about these intractable conditions, and our sessions left me feeling helpless and worn out.

Vocationally, she exhibited numerous strengths, including a strong work ethic, willing attitude, flexibility, and eagerness to please. However, she was extremely sensitive to criticism or slights and was especially susceptible to misunderstandings with superiors or others in authority. Her physical problems and numerous medical appointments required that her employers go to great lengths to accommodate her inconsistent attendance, and her emotional lability required patience and flexibility on the part of her employers.

Dealing with her parents, especially her mother, was one of the more difficult and anxiety-filled areas for Sharon. She sometimes mentions the abuse and incest issues with her father, but that wound seems to have healed, though with a scar. Her relationship with her father is neither close nor comfortable but is usually companionable and lacking in intensity. The burning wound is the neglect and abandonment she feels from her mother, who was unsupportive when the incest was disclosed and is still critical and unempathic. For the longest time, Sharon desperately pursued any sort of nurturing from her mother. When she would get small morsels of attention, she would expect even more and would be devastated when her mother invariably let her down. This pattern of expectation and disillusionment resulted in numerous relapses and was a factor in virtually all of her fourteen admissions to our community crisis residence in the next three years.

In the apartment, Sharon's fear of being alone and need for attention and connection were so great that she often smothered her roommates—they in turn backed away in self-preservation, kicking off a cycle of rivalry, jealousy, and rejection. She had difficulty recognizing and effectively expressing her appropriate anger and sometimes engaged in self-mutilating behaviors.

Throughout our work, she very concretely and plaintively expressed identity and dependency issues with big, unanswerable questions: "What am I going to do with my life? Am I grown up yet? Am I going to get well? Why is God doing this to me? What will happen to me if I get too healthy?" She would say these things in such a heartfelt, earnest way that it was difficult not to try to dig in and really work with her to find immediate answers. Maintaining a neutral tone, I would often agree with her that life is unfair and that her situation was difficult and would express confidence that she would find her own answers. I was often bluntly honest in assessing reality: "It doesn't seem like your parents are going to change much, so you'll have to decide if you want to do things differently with them"; or simply, "I don't have the answer." Overall, it seemed most helpful to focus on the present, allowing Sharon to develop ego strength by mastering current life crises. Spending too much time processing the past seemed to foster regression. This was especially true with regard to her incest experience, and we found it most helpful to focus on how that experience affected her ability to maintain boundaries or develop trust in current relationships.

There were some areas where more directive assistance was helpful. When Sharon experimented with dating, we discussed safety issues and limit setting. We sometimes role-played assertiveness vignettes to assist her in dealing with employers, co-workers, and eventually her parents. I also helped her develop coping techniques, such as compartmentalizing when she was overwhelmed, anticipating and planning for her emotional needs, and using relaxation and self-soothing techniques that allowed her to gain some sense of mastery over everyday stress. Finally, using humor helped her gain perspective on her problems and break her cycle of misery and heaviness.

When I reflect back on our five years together, the incredible amount of telephone contact makes this experience especially distinctive. Sharon did not hesitate to use the phone to meet her seemingly endless need for reassurance and soothing. Although she most often called me, she also frequently called Kanter, our duty therapist, emergency services, church staff and members, and various local hotlines.

I initially tried solving these crises with her, but attempts to calm her down only elicited agitation and resistance. Realizing this was not working, I just started listening empathetically and validating her feelings, with no attempt to help her solve the problem. I would say something like, "Gee, that sounded difficult," or that this seemed to be a tough problem that I did not think had any easy answers, or that the problem probably would not be resolved now or in the near future—asking what she was going to do to take care of herself in the meantime. This respectful but relaxed and noncommittal response to her urgency and anxiety had a calming effect. While I did try to be responsive to her in a timely way, I was also realistic with her about the extent of my availability to her. As I was frequently unavailable when she needed me, she would need to seek other resources and learn to tolerate dysphoric states.

At times, her dependence on me became overwhelming to her and made it difficult for her to express anger directly toward me. For example, she recently called Kanter and told him she wanted to fire me because she "wanted a therapist she could hate." At one point, her frequent calls both to myself and our emergency staff became so burdensome that we developed a plan in which she was to call emergency services every morning at a specific time to report on her daily coping strategies. Additionally, if she was in crisis, she was to call again in the afternoon. This plan acknowledged both her need for phone support and the reality that we could not stop her from calling. By prescribing this support, we hoped to help her feel less needy, desperate, and burdensome. Within a short time, she was complaining that the call-in schedule was too demanding and that it conflicted with her daily activities. She assured me that we could get along without her.

Six months after Sharon moved into her own Section 8 apartment, I transferred from our center's residential program to the case management unit where Kanter worked. This put us on the same unit, and we decided that, since I was doing the majority of the work with Sharon, it would be best to formally transfer the case. He continued to stay involved in a collateral role because she seemed to benefit from involvements with both of us.

On three occasions after the transfer, Kanter joined my meetings with Sharon, when it seemed that the relationship between Sharon and me had become too intense and that Sharon was beginning to regress. Sharon was protective of her time with me and griped about his presence. Our implicit message to her was that if she was doing better, he would not have to come to the session. This approach would quickly dilute her intense maternal transference by reassuring her that her relationship with the clinic was not totally dependent on me.

Sharon's life has objectively improved over the past few years. There is still subjective distress around the same themes, but this distress is less intense, less frequent, and requires a lower level of staff intervention. For the most part, she has been consistently employed on a part-time basis, and recently celebrated the three-year anniversary of living by herself in her own apartment. She has gradually expanded her social network and is learning to engage in more reciprocal friendships, although loneliness continues to be a prominent theme. A series of small house pets has helped in relieving some of the intense loneliness. They seem to have had short life spans or met with fatal mishaps, so Sharon has developed some experience with death and surviving loss. As she begins to get more of her needs met elsewhere and has more realistic expectations of her parents' limited ability to nurture her, she is better able to regulate closeness and distance with them in a way that allows her to maintain a relationship with them but also protects her from their insensitivity and cruelty. Her need for inpatient and crisis residence stabilization has decreased from six instances in 1991, to four in 1992 (including her only inpatient treatment since her 1987 state hospital discharge—two admissions totalling fourteen days), to three in 1993 (one for only one day), to one in 1994. Notably, all of these admissions were voluntary and were not precipitated by life-threatening behavior. These changes occurred slowly and gradually.

Within the past six months, however, a remarkable and dramatic change has occurred. After many attempts to stop smoking, she was finally able to quit this past year. Within weeks, she was off all her asthma medication, antibiotics, painkillers, and high blood pressure medication. She returned her breathing machine to the medical supply company. Without the stimulant effect of inhalers, her moods became more even, and she felt more in control. Agitation and anxiety decreased, and for the first time she was able to sit calmly in a chair for an entire hour. She is sleeping better, and doctor appointments do not interfere with her new job.

One final measure of progress: at a recent session she handed me her billing sheet with a handwritten letter stapled on top. The letter was a litany of things she was angry about, and it started out with: "Barbara, I'm angry with you because you weren't there when I needed you yesterday." As we talked, she was able to describe both her anger and her attachment to me. She does not have to split between Kanter and me anymore. She can tell me directly about her mix of positive and negative feelings toward me. A crowning achievement.

When I met Sharon in the waiting room for our regular meeting most recently, she presented me with a garden pack of four marigolds as a gift. Three had large yellow blooms on them, and one had a bud that had not yet blossomed. As she pointed to each of the yellow flowers, she said: "This one is

Carolyn, this one is Joel, this one is you." Pointing to the bud, she announced that that one represented her. "All the flowers have blossomed, but yours hasn't opened—it's still a bud," I responded. "I know," she said, "but just plant it and it will flower like the rest of them. Don't worry, Barbara, it will blossom."

Discussion

As we contemplate our collective involvement with Sharon over the past thirteen years, Winnicott's (1984) comments to an audience of social workers seem most apt: "Your job is to survive. In this setting the word survive means not only that you live through it and that you manage not to get damaged, but also that you are not provoked into vindictiveness. . . . [Case management] may be a kind of loving but often it has to be a kind of hating and the key word is not treatment or cure but rather it is survival" (pp. 227–228).

Similarly, commenting on the long-term outcome of persons with borderline personality disorder, Francis (1986) has noted that although these clients have a one in seven chance of dying, their disorders often improve dramatically in the second decade. Thus, he identifies the primary goal of professionals working with these individuals as simply helping them remain alive until age thirty. Fortunately, through luck or effort, we were able to accomplish this goal. Although we would like to believe our efforts were more far-reaching, much of our effort over the past thirteen years has been crisis intervention, providing ongoing clinical management that helped Sharon survive until a healing process could develop its own momentum (Kanter, 1985). Although the case report describes various treatment protocols that appear helpful in retrospect, our ongoing anxiety and helplessness cannot be underestimated. To a large extent, the professional challenge in this situation centered on managing our countertransference (Kanter, 1988, 1990; Goldstein, 1991).

On a more prosaic level, this case report also illustrates the central principles of the clinical case management approach: maintaining continuity of care, using the case management relationship, titrating support and structure, maintaining flexibility of intervention strategies, and facilitating client resourcefulness (Kanter, 1989). In the remainder of this discussion, we will briefly examine how each of these principles was operationalized in our work with Sharon.

Continuity of Care. To our knowledge, this is one of the first case reports that has encompassed both community treatment and a relatively long-term tenure in a public mental hospital. Although located over 150 miles from Western State Hospital, our agency has worked closely with hospital staff for many years, combining monthly day-long visits by our liaison worker—a key member of our case management team—with frequent phone contact (Zellmer, Maurer, and Kanter, 1985; Kanter, 1991). In Sharon's situation, this collaboration was facilitated by the fact that same individual (Maurer) was both her case manager and her liaison worker. In this dual role, Maurer was especially qualified to collaborate with the hospital staff in monitoring Sharon's progress in the hospital and in formulating a discharge plan. Later, her personal knowledge of Sharon enabled her to effectively consult with the subsequent case managers when various difficulties arose. Similarly, Barber's discharge summary proved invaluable in helping us extend an effective treatment profile from the hospital into the community.

Several years later, Kanter and Caceres were able to collaborate with each other in transferring clinical responsibility for Sharon as she moved into new residential arrangements and presented changing treatment and case management needs. Finally, though this was not mentioned in our report, we spent much time working with the three psychiatrists (incidentally, all female) on our team who have treated Sharon since her discharge from Western State Hospital. (Owing to space limitations, we did not address the complex psychopharmacological and medical issues in this case in any detail. Sharon has been attentively treated with psychiatric medications from almost every major category; although some have had significant clinical utility, none have produced any dramatic response in her overall clinical status.)

Throughout this case, clinical transitions can be compared to the baton-passing in a relay race, as the clinicians on each leg "ran alongside each other" as clinical responsibility was gently passed on. Too often, these transitions are poorly handled in community support systems. Clinicians and case managers are often content to fulfill administrative requirements for a brief transfer or discharge summary. Essentially, the baton is dropped until some other professional or agency picks it up—and often runs off in a very different direction. These fumbled transitions often severely damage clients and quickly dissipate significant treatment gains.

The Case Management Relationship. As suggested by our report, the case management relationship involves struggle and collaboration, protectiveness and empowerment, dependency and letting go, transference and reality, and loving and hating (Kanter, 1988). Although we occasionally paddled rhythmically with Sharon down a placid river, more often we felt like we were flailing along with her in a raft pummelled by Class Five rapids. Over time, we learned to follow Winnicott's advice for case managers: "in your . . . professional area [you are] deeply involved in feeling, yet at the same time detached in that you know that you have no responsibility for the fact of your client's illness, and you know the limits of your powers to alter a crisis situation. If you can hold the situation together, the possibility is that the crisis will resolve itself" (Winnicott, 1965, p. 229; Kanter, 1990).

This acknowledgement of our considerable helplessness helped us understand that our usual problem-solving approaches rarely worked. When we tried to defend against our helplessness by responding to Sharon's distress with rational advice, she often experienced us as uncaring and intrusive and became more anxious and fragmented. However, if we could contain our countertransference and could listen empathically, she often was able to use us to restore her self-soothing capacities and considerable social skills (Greenberg, 1986; Harris and Bergman, 1987). At times, this process seemed analogous to soothing a colicky infant: quietly holding the child without frantically searching for the proper bottle temperature or formula mixture.

Responding to these emotional needs also involved acknowledging our limitations as professionals with large caseloads and valued personal lives. We could only offer this support in inadequate, symbolic quantities. In the hospital, formal therapy sessions were limited to a half hour weekly (beyond considerable attention from the ward staff); in the community, weekly sessions were accompanied by increasingly time-limited phone calls, in which we would simply tell her that we only had several minutes available or that we "have to stop now"—aware that Sharon's distress would continue. In using this approach, we attempted to avoid exacerbating her considerable shame about her emotional needs by confronting her dependent behaviors.

Throughout Sharon's community tenure, we attempted to support her efforts to expand her support network while allowing a dependent transference to emerge. She was well aware of the real limitations of our availability and consciously struggled to develop interdependent relationships with a wider circle of friends and acquaintances. In many respects, this is the main objective of our ongoing work. Also, we believe that Sharon may benefit from additional group psychotherapy experience, perhaps with other survivors of sexual abuse, where she could learn how to more effectively fulfill her emotional needs from her peers.

Titrating Support and Structure. As Sharon's needs for support and structure varied greatly, a major component of our case management efforts involved helping to locate and sustain environments that would address these changing needs. After observing her pattern of ambitious functioning, relapse, and hospitalization in her early twenties, we learned that Sharon often underestimated her needs for environmental support; thus she was involuntarily hospitalized for nearly two years while she learned more effective coping skills. On discharge, we consciously attempted to extend the hospital structure into the community, voluntarily engaging her cooperation in accepting limitations on competitive employment and independent living for a period of time.

As she became involved in a more stressful lifestyle, Sharon intermittently became anxious and depressed and was responsive to a collaborative exploration of a need for temporary residential support. Because these discussions occurred before she lost control, we were usually able to address these needs by increasing our contact, adjusting her medications, or less frequently, by admitting her voluntarily to our crisis residence or local inpatient service. This capacity to collaborate in titrating psychological, pharmacological, and environmental support was a major change from her functioning before her extended hospitalization.

Flexibility of Intervention Strategy. Although we had more weekly, fifty-minute, office-based sessions with Sharon than we do with many clients in our program, we often had to vary our treatment approach to accommodate changing needs. As indicated, we sometimes met with her more frequently than once weekly and engaged in numerous telephone contacts, especially when she was alone in her own apartment. In other periods, we met with her in her apartment or outside for walks, as she often had trouble sitting still.

Besides these physical issues, we experimented with many clinical strategies, including scheduled daily phone calls and three-way meetings. Also, while we initially resisted her wish to change case managers, we later transferred clinical responsibility as her attachment to Caceres developed and the need for a female case manager became evident. Although our agency uses an individual case management model in its formal structure, we have learned that clients like Sharon require involvement with a team of professionals who can maintain ongoing coverage, dilute dependent attachments, and provide a continuing psychological involvement when negative transferences emerge.

Facilitating Client Resourcefulness. While some have stressed the importance of recognizing client strengths in case management (Rapp, 1993), Sharon's story illustrates the complexities of this approach. We learned that her strengths often led her to become involved in stressful situations that would precipitate relapse. In some ways, the major challenge of this case was helping Sharon to more directly acknowledge her deficits and limitations; in doing so, she was able to more consistently utilize her productive capacities for employment, independent living, and supporting others in her social network.

Interestingly, we sometimes supported her resourcefulness by withholding what might be conventionally viewed as case management assistance. For example, we almost never became involved in helping Sharon secure employment or in consulting with her workplace supervisors. Although she sometimes obtained jobs that proved unsuitable, we deliberately did not refer her for vocational rehabilitation or job coaching as these services would have likely fostered new dependencies in spheres of her life where she functioned autonomously when psychiatrically stable. Instead, we addressed her employment in supportive psychotherapy, assisting her in clarifying and coping with interpersonal stressors and helping her become more skillful in finding employment that provided satisfaction without excessive stress.

Catching our collective breaths, we feel fortunate to have survived this trek with Sharon; she is alive and thriving—though hardly living in a rose garden—and we have all continued to work in public mental health settings where we are still able to enjoy the wildflowers that bloom amid the chaos of imperfect systems and the pain of mental illness. Reflecting on our experience with Sharon over the past two decades, we find ourselves in the position of a team of mountain climbers, momentarily enjoying the view of the valley far below before continuing to trudge on toward the summit far ahead.

References

Francis, A. Lecture on the long-term course of borderline personality disorder at the annual conference of the American Psychiatric Association, Washington, D.C., May 15, 1986.

Goldstein, W. N. "Clarification of Projective Identification." *American Journal of Psychiatry,* 1991, *148* (2), 153–161.

Greenberg, S. "The Supportive Approach to Therapy." *Clinical Social Work Journal,* 1986, *14,* 6–13.

Harris, M., and Bergman, H. C. "Case Management with the Chronically Mentally Ill: A Clinical Perspective." *American Journal of Orthopsychiatry,* 1987, *57* (2), 296–302.

Kanter, J. S. "The Process of Change in the Chronic Mentally Ill: A Naturalistic Perspective." *Psychosocial Rehabilitation Journal,* 1985, *9* (1), 55–69.

Kanter, J. S. "Clinical Issues in the Case Management Relationship." In M. Harris and L. Bachrach (eds.), *Clinical Case Management.* New Directions for Mental Health Services, no. 40. San Francisco: Jossey-Bass, 1988.

Kanter, J. S. "Clinical Case Management: Definition, Principles, Components." *Hospital and Community Psychiatry,* 1989, *40,* 361–368.

Kanter, J. S. "Community-Based Management of Psychotic Clients: The Contributions of D. W. and Clare Winnicott." *Clinical Social Work Journal,* 1990, *18* (1), 23–41.

Kanter, J. S. "Integrating Case Management and Psychiatric Hospitalization." *Health and Social Work,* 1991, *16* (1), 34–42.

Rapp, C. "Theory, Principles and Methods of the Strengths Model of Case Management." In M. Harris and H. C. Bergman (eds.), *Case Management for Mentally Ill Patients.* Langhorne, Pa.: Harwood, 1993.

Winnicott, D. W. *Maturational Processes and the Facilitating Environment.* New York: International Universities Press, 1965.

Winnicott, D. W. *Delinquency and Deprivation.* London: Tavistock, 1984.

Zellmer, D., Maurer, C. L., and Kanter, J. S. "Treating the Whole Elephant: Delivering Comprehensive Services to the Chronic Mentally Ill." In J. S. Kanter (ed.), *Clinical Issues in Treating the Chronic Mentally Ill.* New Directions for Mental Health Services, no. 27. San Francisco: Jossey-Bass, 1985.

BARBARA ZIMMANN CACERES, M.S.W., L.C.S.W., is a case manager on the community support services unit at Mount Vernon Center for Community Mental Health, Fairfax County, Virginia.

JOEL KANTER, M.S.W., L.C.S.W., is a senior case manager on the community support services unit at Mount Vernon Center for Community Mental Health, Fairfax County, Virginia.

JACK BARBER, M.D., is medical director of Western State Hospital in Staunton, Virginia, and associate professor of psychiatric medicine at the University of Virginia School of Medicine.

CAROLYN MAURER, M.S.W., L.C.S.W., is coordinator of the community support services unit at Mount Vernon Center for Community Mental Health, Fairfax County, Virginia.

Commentary

Robert W. Surber, M.S.S.W.
Deputy Chief of Community Services
Department of Psychiatry
San Francisco General Hospital

One of the premises of clinical case management is that significant change occurs through the relationship between the individual and the case manager (Surber, 1994). This story of Sharon demonstrates both the struggles and the growth that these relationships can engender for clients and treaters alike.

This story is one that is common in public mental health services. Numerous individuals are repeatedly admitted to the hospital with multiple or unclear diagnoses, multiple problems and limited capacity to find or use available resources, and tumultuous relationships with literally everyone with whom they come into contact (Surber and others, 1987).

Evidence is mounting that a large number of these individuals have suffered from repeated abuse and that for women in particular this often includes a history of sexual abuse and trauma. Treatment must be tailored to respond to the needs brought forth by this abuse (Harris, 1994). Most often, treaters do not even assess the degree or type of abuse and trauma or the impact on the individual's development and relationships. Thus past abuse is often ignored in treatment (Jennings, 1994). Yet repeated abuse and trauma and the emotional neglect that frequently accompanies them can have a devastating impact on an individual's ability to establish and maintain the interdependent relationships that are necessary to function, pursue goals, and find meaning in life.

The case management relationship is often a necessary tool in helping individuals develop the capacity to relate. In describing the value of this relationship, Balancio states, "It is considered that a positive connection is therapeutic in itself. Improvements in the capacity to bond facilitate adaptation. The relationship becomes the 'sustaining link' between a client and an external world which is often experienced as confusing and chaotic. It allows for identification and internalization to occur, processes that help a client form a sense of self" (1994, p. 25).

It appears from the description of this case that the relationships between Sharon and her treaters have indeed fostered her ability to bond and have provided a safe link to an apparently chaotic and hostile world. Through these relationships, she also seems to be developing an enhanced sense of herself. But it has not been easy, for anyone.

By definition, a relationship involves two people: two people who touch each other's lives. For the relationship to have an impact on Sharon's life, her treaters must be touched by her depression, her emptiness, her loneliness, her anxiety, and her rage. During much of the time that this work occurred, these may have been the only expressions of her spirit she could manifest.

The point is that being emotionally touched by the client is necessary to form an attachment or bond, that an attachment is necessary to facilitate the client's capacity to relate (Bowlby, 1973), and that the client's increased ability to relate will foster the ability to pursue goals and develop meaningful activities.

Being touched by a client's pain can bring about many of the same feelings of anger and hopelessness that the client feels. In clinical terms this is called countertransference. When it is so powerful that it can no longer be tolerated it is described as burnout. Case managers and other treaters require considerable support and understanding to manage and appreciate the impact of countertransference in their work. Otherwise, they are prone to reject the client and reinforce the client's feelings of worthlessness—or to leave the field altogether. This support is provided through supervisors, colleagues, educational activities, and vacations provided by the treatment program, and by family, friends, and spiritual and other restorative opportunities elsewhere. This support, which is also provided largely through relationships, is as important to case managers as the case managers' support is to the clients.

Managing the feelings that arise for case managers in the relationship also requires considerable skill and sound clinical judgment. Much of the work described in this case runs counter to what one might normally think of as usual practice for case managers. This includes being relatively inflexible to changing an established treatment plan, resisting a flight to health and requiring the client to push through the resistance, and taking a detached stance toward the client's expression of pain. The essence of case management, however, is to provide what is needed for the client and for the relationship between the client and case manager. Understanding and implementing what is needed is aided by knowledge, skill, judgment, intuition, trial and error, and luck.

For Sharon, and others like her, the maintenance of the relationship is the most critical aspect of care (Fariello and Powers, 1994). This is so for two reasons. The first derives from the principle of continuity of care, of which one aspect is that case management programs cannot quit being available to serve their clients. Clients, of course, can quit the programs—repeatedly if they wish. Nevertheless, the program must stand ready and available to assist the client when (and if) the client is willing. If not, there is no hope for the program to help the client improve (Surber, 1994). This does not mean that individual case managers must stick with a situation they cannot manage. As in this case, the program must also provide adequate support to the case manager in terms of realistic expectations. It must also be prepared to send in reinforcements, providing increased structure through hospitalization of the client or the involvement of other clinicians.

The second reason is that the client behaviors, and the reactions elicited in the case management relationship, are likely to be very similar to those in the other relationships of the client's life, which are not infrequently disastrous. The case management relationship offers one of the only opportunities for many clients to develop an effective and meaningful interdependent relationship, which can also help them develop the capacity to establish interdependent relationships with others and begin to create a natural support system.

Are these interdependent relationships? Clients certainly depend on case managers for care, treatment, and support. But case managers also depend on clients, if only for a job, an income, and a career. Through the relationship, case managers also join the clients in the struggles of this life, to find purpose and meaningful activities, to love and be loved, and to survive. It is clear from the telling of this story that case managers feel the pain and share the joy along with their clients. In doing so, case managers are helped to find their own answers to these struggles and, through these interdependent relationships, to grow along with their clients.

Once in a while, there is an opportunity to take a moment to smell the flowers and enjoy the view before continuing on in the struggle.

Commentary References

Balancio, E. F., "Clinical Case Management." In R. W. Surber (ed.), *Clinical Case Management: A Guide to Comprehensive Treatment of Serious Mental Illness*. Newbury Park, Calif.: Sage, 1994.

Bowlby, J. *Attachment and Loss*. Vol. 2: *Separation: Anxiety and Anger*. New York: Basic Books, 1973.

Fariello, D. F., and Powers, S. "Clinical Case Management of Personality Disordered Clients." In R. W. Surber (ed.), *Clinical Case Management: A Guide to Comprehensive Treatment of Serious Mental Illness*. Newbury Park, Calif.: Sage, 1994.

Harris, M. "Modifications in Service Delivery and Clinical Treatment for Women Diagnosed with Severe Mental Illness Who Are Also the Survivors of Sexual Abuse Trauma." *Journal of Mental Health Administration*, 1994, 2 (4), 397–406.

Jennings, A. "On Being Invisible in the Mental Health System." *Journal of Mental Health Administration*, 1994, 2 (4), 374–385.

Surber, R. W. "An Approach to Care." In R. W. Surber (ed.), *Clinical Case Management: A Guide to Comprehensive Treatment of Serious Mental Illness*. Newbury Park, Calif.: Sage, 1994.

Surber, R. W., Winkler, E. L., Montelsone, M., Havassy, B. E., Goldfinger, S. M., and Hopkin, J. T. "Characteristics of High Users of Acute Psychiatric Inpatient Services." *Hospital and Community Psychiatry*, 1987, 38, 1112–1114.

INDEX

Abandonment issues, 82, 97
Abstinence: motivating client toward, 55, 62; using confinement to enforce, 43–44. *See also* Relapse prevention
Abstinence-oriented homes, 54, 63
Affect stimulation, in group treatment, 64
Alcoholics Anonymous (AA), 54
Alcohol, enforced abstinence from, to assess schizophrenic, 43–44
Alcoholism: in homeless schizophrenic man, 37–50; as primary diagnosis, 40–41. *See also* Abstinence; Dual-diagnosis clients; Substance abuse
Alone, fear of being, 75, 97
Anderson, C. M., 35
Anger, 31, 37, 98
Anxiety: about being alone, 75, 97; in therapy sessions, 72, 73, 75
Approach-avoidance dilemma, 82
Arrest, to prevent death, 41–42
Ashikago, T., 3
Assertive community treatment: dilemmas of, 45–46, 47; for dual-diagnosis clients, 37–50, 62; limitations of, 45–46
Assertiveness training program, 74
Atkinson, D., 20
Attachment. *See* Dependent attachment
Auditory hallucinations, 54, 56, 92
Autonomy: vs. coercive control, 2, 46, 55–56, 63, 65, 66–68; and relapse, 79; for sexual abuse survivors, 84, 85, 86. *See also* Coercive interventions; Independence

Barber, J., 2, 89–107
Bartels, S. J., 61, 68
Bebout, R. R., 53, 61
Bennett, M. J., 19, 49
Bergman, H. C., 1, 3, 53, 81, 101
Bernheim, K. F., 30, 36
Borderline personality disorder: and case manager role, 81; in case studies, 71–86, 89–107; crisis intervention for, 100; as diagnostic category, 71; externally focused activity in, 77; and limited time, 102; long-term outcome of, 100; medical problems in, 96; regression in, 91, 92, 97, 98; splitting in, 84, 91, 99;

stigmatization of, 71, 85. *See also* Shannon case study; Sharon case study
Boundary flexibility, 18, 35, 39–40, 79, 81. *See also* Friendship
Boyd, J. L., 35
Breeding, K. A., 50
Breier, A., 3
Brooks, G. W., 3
Brotman, A., 63
Brown, G., 19
Burnout, case worker, 91, 93. *See also* Countertransference

Caceres, B. Z., 2, 89–107
Case management: of assertive community treatment for dual-diagnosis client, 37–50; with community and hospital collaboration, 89–107; family-centered, 23–36; friendship vs. professional activity in, 5–20; importance of, for nonpsychotic clients, 81; integrated psychotherapeutic and environmental interventions in, 71–86; of multifaceted treatment approach, with dual-diagnosis client, 53–69; practice vs. policy in, 1; problem-focus vs. longer-term focus in, 1; for trauma survivors, 85
Case management relationship: long-term, with borderline client, 101–102; in multifaceted treatment approach, 61–62; multiple interpersonal dimensions of, 68. *See also* Countertransference; Dependent attachment; Therapeutic relationship
Case manager: gender of, for sexual abuse survivors, 86, 93, 96; limitation of, to environmental interventions, 82; role of, as family consultant, 23–36; role of, for both environmental interventions and psychodynamic work, 81–82; support for, 86, 100. *See also* Countertransference; Dependent attachment
Clark, R. E., 61, 68
Clubhouse programs, 74, 77, 78
Coercive interventions: abuse of, 68, 86; for dual-diagnosis clients, 41–46, 48–49, 65, 66–67; for suicidal trauma survivors, 86; vs. unconditional/supportive

109

Ordering Information

NEW DIRECTIONS FOR MENTAL HEALTH SERVICES is a series of paperback books that presents timely and readable volumes on subjects of concern to clinicians, administrators, and others involved in the care of the mentally disabled. Each volume is devoted to one topic and includes a broad range of authoritative articles written by noted specialists in the field. Books in the series are published quarterly in Spring, Summer, Fall, and Winter and are available for purchase by subscription as well as individually.

SUBSCRIPTIONS for 1995 cost $56.00 for individuals (a savings of 20 percent over single-copy prices) and $78.00 for institutions, agencies, and libraries. Please do not send institutional checks for personal subscriptions. Standing orders are accepted.

SINGLE COPIES cost $17.95 when payment accompanies order. (California, New Jersey, New York, and Washington, D.C., residents please include appropriate sales tax.) All orders will be charged postage and handling.

DISCOUNTS FOR QUANTITY ORDERS are available. Please write to the address below for information.

ALL ORDERS must include either the name of an individual or an official purchase order number. Please submit your order as follows:
    Subscriptions: specify series and year subscription is to begin
    Single copies: include individual title code (such as MHS59)

MAIL ALL ORDERS TO:
    Jossey-Bass Publishers
    350 Sansome Street
    San Francisco, California 94104-1342

FOR SUBSCRIPTION SALES OUTSIDE OF THE UNITED STATES, contact any international subscription agency or Jossey-Bass directly.

OTHER TITLES AVAILABLE IN THE
NEW DIRECTIONS FOR MENTAL HEALTH SERVICES SERIES
H. Richard Lamb, Editor-in-Chief